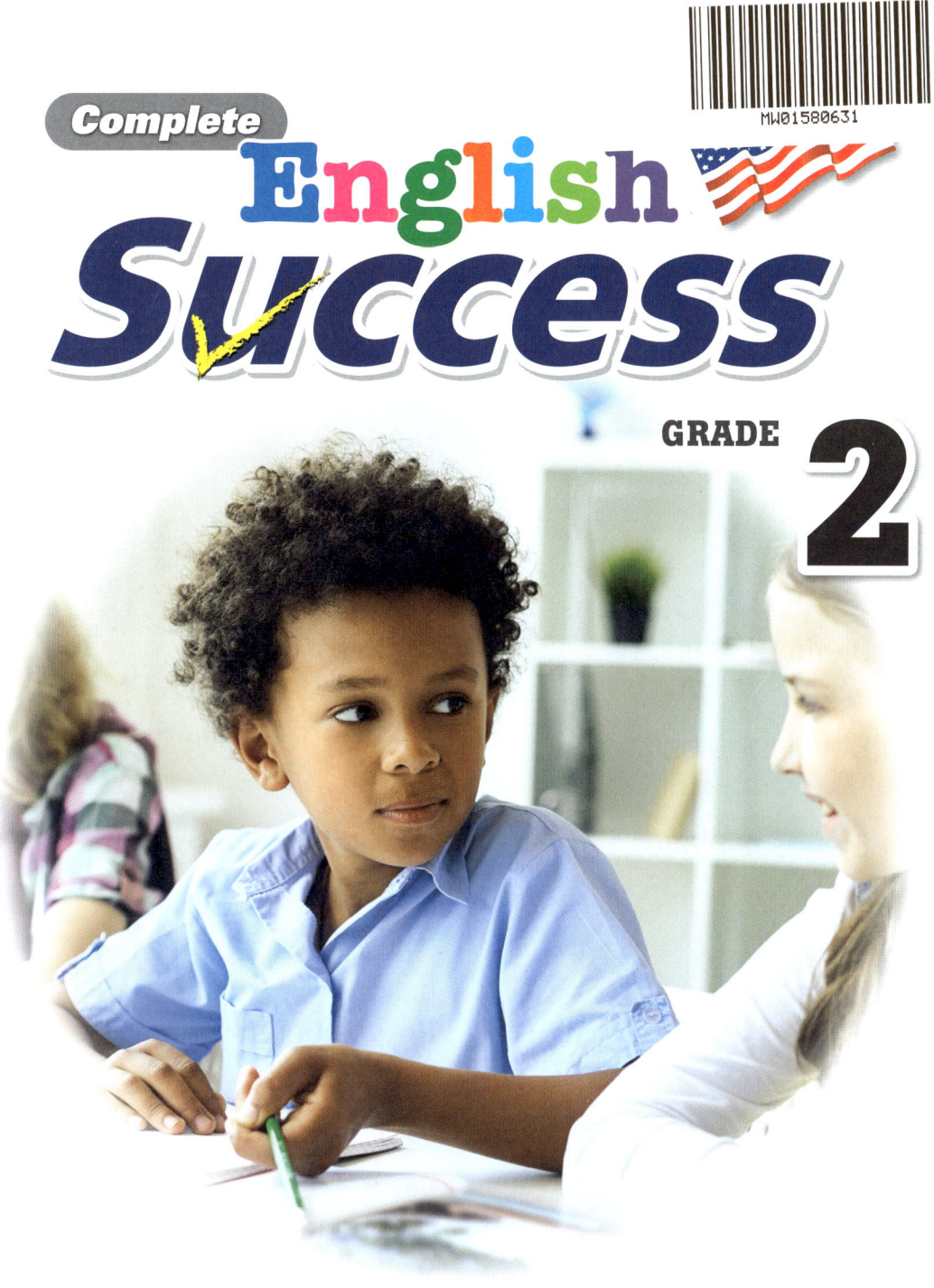

ISBN: 978-1-942830-60-3

Complete English Success

2022 First Edition

Copyright © 2022 Popular Book Company (USA) Limited

All rights reserved. No part of this publication may be reproduced, stored in a retrieval system, or transmitted in any form or by any means, electronic, mechanical, photocopying, recording or otherwise, without the prior written permission of the Publisher, Popular Book Company (USA) Limited.

Printed in China

| Section 1 | Phonics |

Unit 1 — 6 – 9
Consonants

Unit 2 — 10 – 13
Hard and Soft "c" and "g"

Unit 3 — 14 – 17
Silent Consonants

Unit 4 — 18 – 21
Consonant Blends: L Blends

Unit 5 — 22 – 25
Consonant Blends: R Blends

Unit 6 — 26 – 29
Consonant Blends: S Blends

Unit 7 — 30 – 33
Consonant Digraphs

Unit 8 — 34 – 37
Short Vowels

Unit 9 — 38 – 41
Long Vowels

Unit 10 — 42 – 45
Y as a Vowel

Unit 11 — 46 – 49
Vowel Digraphs

Unit 12 — 50 – 53
Vowel Digraph: oo

Unit 13 — 54 – 57
Diphthongs

Unit 14 — 58 – 61
Rhyming Words

Review 1 — 62 – 67

| Section 2 | Grammar |

Unit 1 — 70 – 73
Nouns

Unit 2 — 74 – 77
Articles

Unit 3 — 78 – 81
Pronouns

Unit 4 — 82 – 85
Present Tense Verbs

Unit 5 — 86 – 89
Past Tense Verbs

Unit 6 — 90 – 93
Adjectives

Unit 7 — 94 – 97
Prepositions

Unit 8 — 98 – 101
Joining Words

Unit 9 — 102 – 105
The Sentence: Subject and Predicate

Unit 10 — 106 – 109
Subjects and Objects

Unit 11 — 110 – 113
Types of Sentences

Unit 12 — 114 – 117
Punctuation and Capitalization

Contents

Grade 2

Unit 13 Forming Negative Sentences	118 – 121
Unit 14 Contractions	122 – 125
Review 2	126 – 131

Section 3 — Vocabulary

Unit 1 Sense Words	134 – 137
Unit 2 Season Words	138 – 141
Unit 3 Camping Words	142 – 145
Unit 4 Community Words	146 – 149
Unit 5 Polygon Words	150 – 153
Unit 6 Computer Words	154 – 157
Unit 7 Water Words	158 – 161
Unit 8 Synonyms	162 – 165
Unit 9 Antonyms	166 – 169
Unit 10 Homophones	170 – 173
Review 3	174 – 179

Section 4 — Reading and Writing

Unit 1 A Balloon Ride	182 – 185
Unit 2 The Sun and the Ocean	186 – 189
Unit 3 The Museum Trip	190 – 193
Unit 4 Alphabet Rhyme	194 – 197
Unit 5 Today Is My Birthday!	198 – 201
Unit 6 The Butterfly's Life Cycle	202 – 205
Unit 7 Crispy Squares	206 – 209
Unit 8 Jumbo the Gigantic Elephant	210 – 213
Unit 9 Bat Facts	214 – 217
Unit 10 Big Red Rescuer	218 – 221
Review 4	222 – 227

Answers	229 – 258
Language Games	259 – 272

Dear Parent/Guardian,

Thank you for choosing our *Complete English Success* as your child's learning companion.

We are confident that *Complete English Success* is the ultimate supplementary workbook your child needs to build his or her English language skills.

Complete English Success explores the fundamental aspects of language development – phonics (Grades 1 to 3), listening comprehension (Grades 4 to 6), grammar, vocabulary, reading, and writing – by introducing each concept with an easy-to-understand definition and clear examples. This is followed by a variety of interesting activities to provide plenty of practice for your child. There is also a note box at the end of each unit for your child to note down what he or she has learned.

To further ensure that your child retains the language concepts and enjoys the material, there is a review at the end of each section and a Language Games section at the end of the book to help your child consolidate the language concepts in a fun and meaningful way.

Additionally, the QR codes in the book allow quick access to our online audio clips for the Phonics or Listening Comprehension section, which provide a fun way for your child to learn phonics and develop listening skills, and motion graphics that explain key concepts in the English language.

We hope that your child will have fun learning and developing his or her English language skills with our *Complete English Success*.

Your Partner in Education,
Popular Book Company (USA) Limited

 Scan this QR code or go to Download Center at **www.popularbookusa.com** to enjoy more learning fun with our online audio clips and videos!

Section 1

Phonics

Scan this QR code or go to Download Center at **www.popularbookusa.com** to listen to our audio clips on phonics!

 Units 1 – 3
Consonants

 Units 4 – 6
Consonant Blends

 Unit 7
Consonant Digraphs

 Units 8 – 10
Vowels

 Units 11 – 12
Vowel Digraphs

 Unit 13
Diphthongs

 Unit 14
Rhyming Words

Section 1 Phonics

UNIT 1 Consonants

 A consonant is the sound of a letter in a word that is not a vowel (a, e, i, o, or u). It can be at the beginning, in the middle, or at the end of a word.

A. Say the things. Then circle the correct consonants.

1.1 Beginning Consonant

sun
leaf
pan

Beginning Consonant

bat   fish   duck

1.2 Middle Consonant

wa**t**er
shi**v**er
co**r**al

Middle Consonant

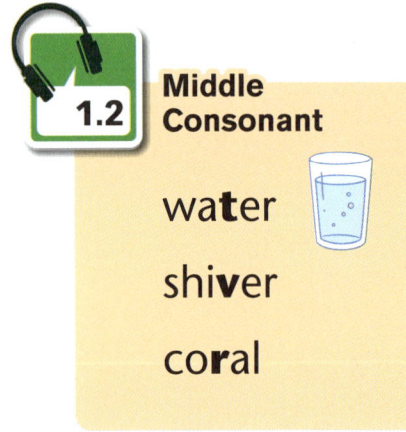   

koala   petal   banana

1.3 Ending Consonant

po**t**
bo**x**
dro**p**

Ending Consonant

bus   pen   jar

B. Say the things and write the words. Then check to show the beginning, middle, and ending consonants.

One of them has two check marks!

Section 1   Unit 1

C. Say the things. Then write the correct beginning, middle, and ending consonants.

Beginning Consonant

__ouse

__ueen

__urtle

__urse

Middle Consonant

I love playing hoc__ey!

bea__er

fai__y

Ending Consonant

STO__

This is a good boo__ .

D. Read the passage and circle the letter "n" in the words with the specified colors.

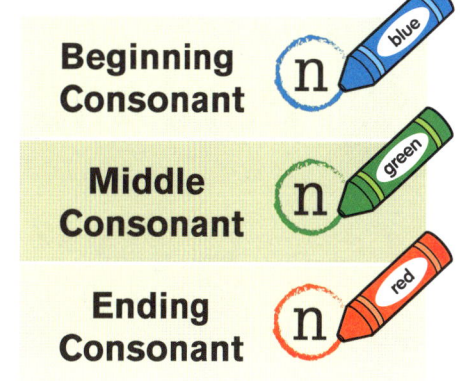

Alaska

Alaska is our largest and northernmost state. It is near the North Pole so it is very cold there. Despite the cold weather, many animals such as polar bears and moose call Alaska home.

In Alaska, there are two months of darkness and two months of daylight. You might see the sun shining at nine o'clock at night in June, just like it does at noon!

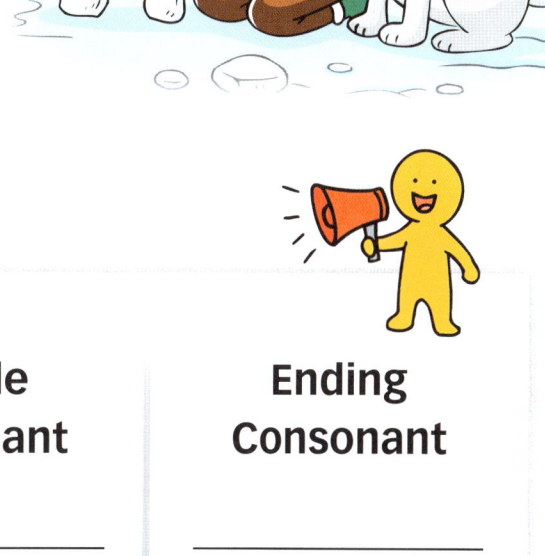

Words That I Have Learned

Beginning Consonant	Middle Consonant	Ending Consonant
_____	_____	_____
_____	_____	_____
_____	_____	_____
_____	_____	_____

Complete English Success (Grade 2)

Section 1 Phonics

UNIT 2 Hard and Soft "c" and "g"

💡 The letters "c" and "g" have both hard and soft sounds.

A. Say the things. Write "c" or "g." Then draw lines to match.

🎧 2.1

c

hard
comb
magi**c**

soft
cent
fa**c**e

1. atti___ 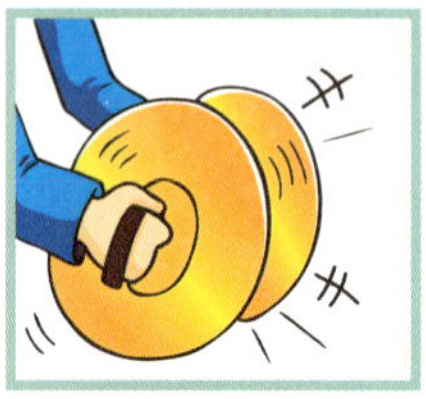   ___ymbals 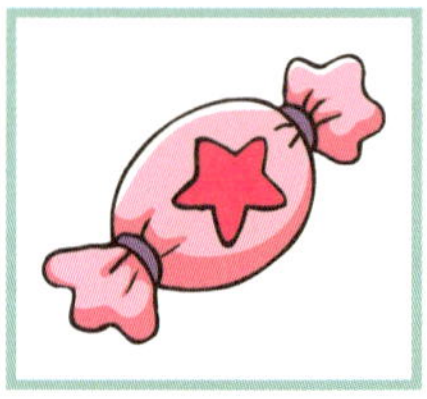   ___andy

   hard "c"   soft "c"

🎧 2.2

g

hard
gate
ta**g**

soft
ginger
oran**g**e

2. an___el    ___irl    fla___

   hard "g"   soft "g"

10   Complete English Success (Grade 2)

B. Say the words under the pictures and write "c" or "g" to show what sounds the words contain. Then name the things that contain the same sounds.

| gift | castle | giraffe | dancer |

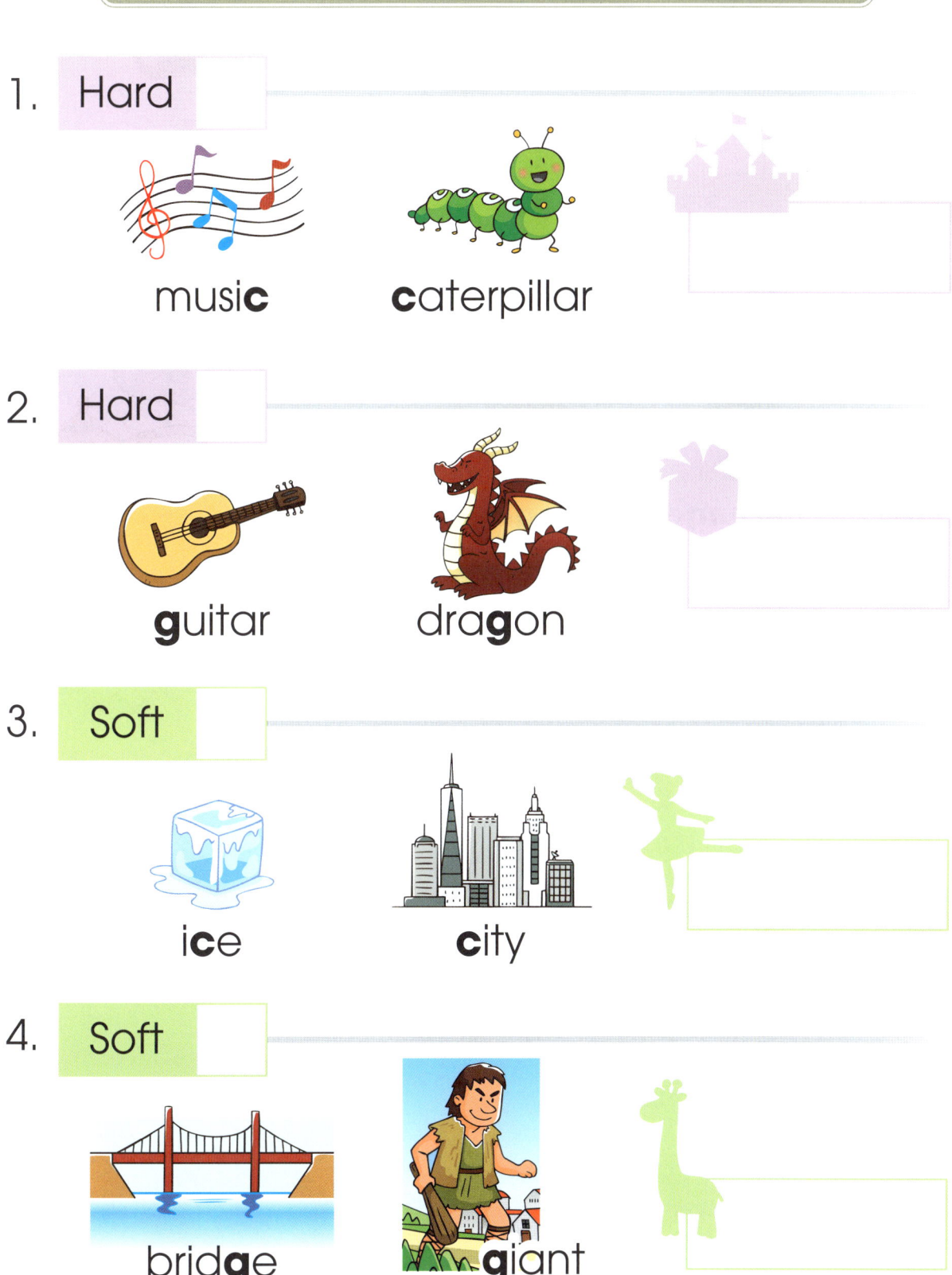

1. Hard [g]
   music   caterpillar   castle

2. Hard [g]
   guitar   dragon   gift

3. Soft [c]
   ice   city   dancer

4. Soft [g]
   bridge   giant   giraffe

C. Say the things. Then write the words in the correct boxes.

D. **Read the passage and circle the letters in the words with the specified colors.**

Penguins

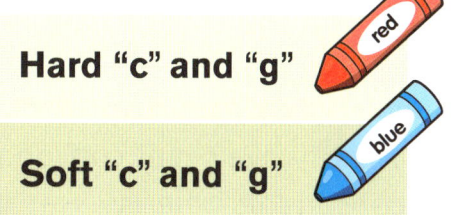

Hard "c" and "g"
Soft "c" and "g"

Penguins are birds that cannot fly but are good swimmers. They live in icy Antarctica and off the coast of Africa and Australia. The smallest penguin is about 13 inches tall. It is called the blue penguin. The tallest penguin, the emperor, seems huge in comparison!

The female penguin lays an egg or two and goes off in search of food. While she is gone, the male protects the eggs from danger.

Words That I Have Learned

Hard "c"	Soft "c"	Hard "g"	Soft "g"
_____	_____	_____	_____
_____	_____	_____	_____
_____	_____	_____	_____
_____	_____	_____	_____

Section 1 Phonics

UNIT 3

Silent Consonants

 Some words have silent consonants. We do not hear the sound of these consonants when we say the words.

A. Say the words. Then circle the silent consonants.

 **Silent Consonants**

b
thum**b**
dou**b**t

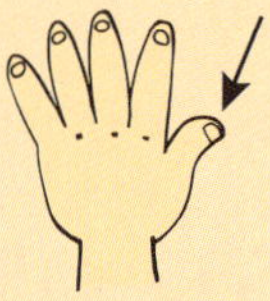

h
g**h**ost
hour

k
knife
knee

l
sa**l**mon
pa**l**m

1.  talk
2.  stalk
3.  crumb
4.  knight
5.  spaghetti
6.  climb
7.  knot
8.  anchor

14 Complete English Success (Grade 2)

B. Trace the letters. Then circle the pictures that contain the given silent consonants.

Silent

comb   plumber   bottle

Silent

whale

hotel

wheat

Silent

knit

kite

Silent

walk   calf   lamp

Section 1 Unit 3

C. Say the things. Then write the silent b, h, k, and l consonants.

1. cha__k
2. __nob
3. sc__ool
4. lam__
5. yo__k

D. Say the words and circle the silent consonants. Then fill in the blanks with the correct words.

honest   calm   knock   choir

1. The words "_____" and "truthful" have similar meanings.

2. _____ before you enter a room.

3. You should remain _____ in an emergency.

4. Ava is a member of the school _____ .

E. Read the story and circle the words with the silent b, h, k, and l consonants.

Kelvin the Knight

Kelvin was an honorable knight. He was charged with capturing the thieving ghosts called Creepie and Spook. At first, Kelvin thought he would lure them with crumbs or salmon, but he knew they were not that dumb. Then he came up with another scheme. He knitted a web and calmly waited for the ghosts to arrive. They got caught in his trap and Kelvin was declared the heir to the throne.

Words That I Have Learned

Words with the Silent b, h, k, and l Consonants

_____

_____

_____

_____

Section 1 Phonics

UNIT 4 Consonant Blends: L Blends

 A consonant blend is a blended sound usually formed by two consonants that are placed together. The L blends are blends that contain the consonant "l."

A. Say the things. Then write the correct L blends.

L Blends

black

clown

flag

glad

plane

sleep

1. __ __ock
2. __ __ock
3. __ __ouse
4. __ __ower
5. __ __ate
6. __ __ake
7. __ __ippers
8. __ __oves

18 Complete English Success (Grade 2)

B. Say the things. Then draw lines to match them with the correct L blends.

C. Write the missing L blends to complete the words.

> bl　cl　fl　gl　pl　sl

1. The ____ass broke into many pieces.

2. There is an American ____ag outside our school.

3. At recess, we ____ay outside.

4. The heavy rain caused many ____oods.

5. "May I have some more, ____ease?" Ani asked.

6. ____oss and brush your teeth regularly.

7. I put jam on a ____ice of bread for breakfast.

8. Although the turtle was ____ow, he won the race because he did his best!

9.

Sharon ____ows the candles when we ____ap.

D. Read the passage and circle the L-blend words.

Ladybugs

Ladybugs are insects. They are often red with black spots. Some are black with red spots. In the summer, they live on flowers, shrubs, and other plants. In the winter, they live in trees and houses.

Ladybugs are capable of flying. Although they cannot reach the clouds, they can reach great heights. On land, they are small enough to crawl on flowers and even on tiny blades of grass!

Words That I Have Learned

L-blend Words

_____

_____

_____

_____

_____

Section 1 | Phonics

UNIT 5

Consonant Blends: R Blends

 The R blends are consonant blends that contain the consonant "r."

A. Say the things. Then write the correct R blends.

R Blends

- **br**ick
- **cr**ab
- **dr**um
- **fr**uit
- **gr**ass
- **pr**ize
- **tr**ee

1.  __ __ayon
2. 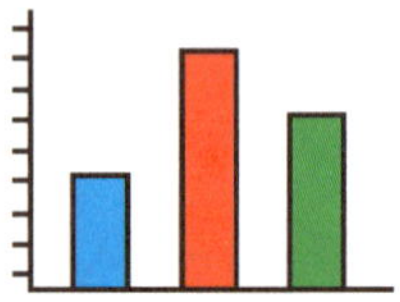 __ __aph
3.  __ __op
4.  __ __og
5.  __ __oom
6.  __ __ash
7.  __ __ince
   __ __ain
   __ __ack

B. Say the things and circle the pictures with R blends. Then write the R blends in the boxes.

R Blends

| br | cr | dr | fr | gr | pr | tr |

Section 1 **Unit 5**

C. Say the things. Check the circles if the words begin with the correct R blends. If not, put a cross and write the correct spellings.

1. **cr**y ◯ _____
2. **dr**ead ◯ _____
3. **tr**ust ◯ _____
4. **dr**ess ◯ _____
5. **cr**ush ◯ _____
6. **pr**ay ◯ _____

D. Say the words and circle the R blends. Then fill in the blanks with the correct words.

crops   Friday   trip   president

1. We are excited to go on our _____ !

2. The farmer takes care of his _____ .

3. I have an appointment on _____ .

4. The _____ made a long speech.

24   Complete English Success (Grade 2)

E. Read the story and circle the R-blend words.

Trisha's Dream

A few days ago, Trisha had a dreadful dream. She was standing under some tall trees in a scary forest. She suddenly felt huge drops of rain on her dress! Trisha ran in the wet grass to hide inside a small brick house. It was then that she woke up to realize that, in reality, there was rain coming in from her window!

Words That I Have Learned

R-blend Words

_____

_____

_____

_____

_____

Section 1 Phonics

UNIT 6 Consonant Blends: S Blends

 The S blends are consonant blends that contain the consonant "s."

A. Trace the S blends. Then say the words.

S Blends (6.1)
- **sc**oop
- **sk**ates
- **sl**ide
- **sm**iley
- **sn**ake
- **sp**ider
- **st**ain
- **sw**ings 

1.  scale
2. 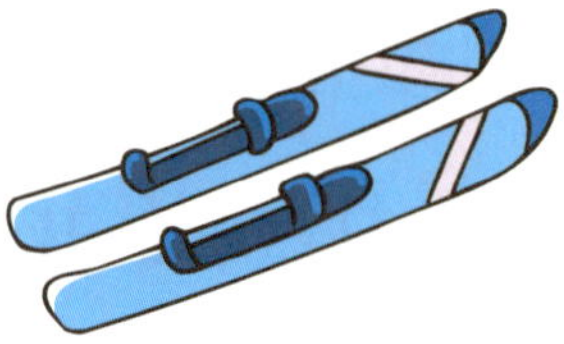 skis
3.  sled
4.  smell
5.  snow
6. 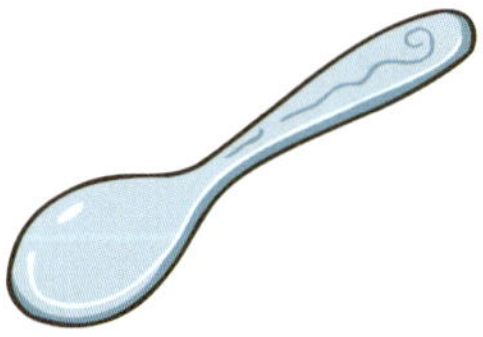 spoon
7.  star
8.  sweep

26 Complete English Success (Grade 2)

B. **Say the words and circle the S blends. Then draw lines to match the words with the pictures.**

S-blend Words

- sponge
- snail
- steam
- switch
- skirt
- scarf

C. **Color the correct S blends.**

1. Martha ⬚sl⬚ ⬚sn⬚ ipped on the floor.
2. The turtle was ⬚sl⬚ ⬚st⬚ ower than the hare.
3. Ana loved the ⬚sn⬚ ⬚sm⬚ all newborn kittens.
4. Cinderella used to ⬚sw⬚ ⬚st⬚ eep the castle floors.
5. The firefighter saw the ⬚sm⬚ ⬚sw⬚ oke from the window.
6. Oh, no! There's a ⬚st⬚ ⬚sk⬚ unk by the tree.

Complete English Success (Grade 2)

Section 1 Unit 6

D. Say the S-blend words. Then label the pictures with the words.

S-blend Words

stairs　spot　smoothie　spade　smell
scooter　snowman　skip　swan　scarf

1. spade / snowman / scarf
2. smoothie
3. smell
4. spot
5. stairs
6. swan
7. scooter
8. skip

E. Read the story and circle the S-blend words.

Dance Lessons

When Stella was three years old, she started taking dance lessons. She wore a pink skirt with small ballet slippers. She practiced the steps every day.

By the time she was 16, she was very good at ballet. Stella was offered the leading role in a play called "Swan." She quickly learned many new steps and routines. Because of her hard work, Stella spun in circles and slowly bowed as she became the star of the stage!

Words That I Have Learned

S-blend Words

_____

_____

_____

_____

Section 1 | Phonics

UNIT 7 Consonant Digraphs

 A consonant digraph is a group of consonants that makes only one sound. "Ch," "sh," "th," and "wh" are consonant digraphs.

A. Write the consonant digraphs ch, sh, th, and wh. Then say the words.

7.1 Consonant Digraphs

ch
chair
cheese

sh
shampoo
sheep

th
thread
thumb

wh
wheel
whistle

ree

eek

istle

T-   irt

orts

oe

30   Complete English Success (Grade 2)

B. Say the things. Then write the correct consonant digraphs in the circles with the help of the words below.

Consonant Digraphs

ch	**sh**	**th**	**wh**
chicks **ch**ild	**sh**ark **sh**ower	**th**ief **th**orn	**wh**iskers **wh**ite

1.

2.

3.

4.

5.

6.

Ouch!

7.

Section 1   Unit 7

C. **Read the tongue twisters and circle the consonant digraphs with the specified colors.**

| Consonant Digraphs | ch (blue)   sh (orange)   th (yellow)   wh (green) |

1. She sells seashells by the seashore.
2. Chester chewed the chewing gum cheerily.
3. The shiny shoes in Susie's Shoe Shop shimmer in the shining sun.
4. Theodore thought the thimble was thick.
5. The thin thief threw the thread to the other three thieves.
6. Willy the Whale whirled while the wheel of the white whaler whistled.

D. **Say the things and write the correct consonant digraphs in the circles. Then give one more example for each.**

My Examples _____

My Examples _____

_____

_____

Complete English Success (Grade 2)

E. Read and underline the consonant digraphs ch, sh, th, and wh.

Sheila's Shopping Adventure

Sheila was excited to go shopping with her elder brother, Chandler. She woke up early on Thursday and showered quickly. Then she threw on her favorite pink dress with white shoes. She was going to buy things for everyone: shampoo for her dog, red thread with a shiny thistle for her grandma, delicious cherries for her mom, and a whistle to surprise Chandler.

However, once they started the car, they noticed that its steering wheel was not working. So they took the bus instead. Sheila saw a big cheese factory, a giant chair, and a whale museum on her way to the mall!

Words That I Have Learned

Consonant Digraphs

_____

_____

_____

Section 1 Phonics

UNIT 8 Short Vowels

💡 Some words with the letter a, e, i, o, or u have the short vowel sounds.

A. Say the words. Then circle the short vowels.

Short Vowels

a — cat 
e — web 
i — bin 
o — clock 
u — jug

1.  net
2.  lamp
3.  tent
4.  six
5.  bug
6.  map
7.  mop
8.  sun
9.  lips
10.  rock

34 Complete English Success (Grade 2)

B. **Say the things. Then color the ones with the short vowel sound for each group.**

Short Vowels

1.

2.

3.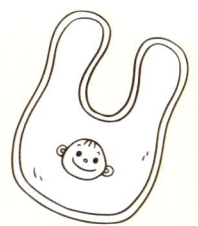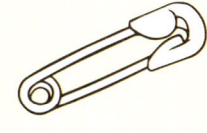

4.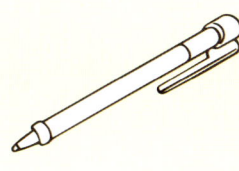

5.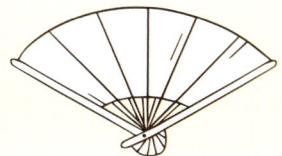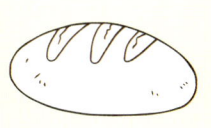

Complete English Success (Grade 2)

Section 1   Unit 8

C. Say the things. Then write the short vowel sound for each.

D. Fill in the blanks with the correct short vowels.

1. A fox lives in a d____n.

2. My d____d took me for a swim.

3. I gave Mom a big h____g for baking me a cake.

4. The ducks were playing in the p____nd.

5. Amy and her tw____n sister look alike.

E. Read the story and circle the underlined short-vowel words with the specified colors.

Jill's Umbrella Hat

Jill has an umbrella hat. It is an umbrella, but it is also a hat. It was a gift from her mom. She can use it in the rain and also in the sun. She wears it on her head. Ron likes her umbrella hat too. He thinks it is fun to wear it.

Short Vowels

a — red
e — blue
i — yellow
o — green
u — purple

Words That I Have Learned

Short-vowel Words

a _____

e _____

i _____

o _____

u _____

Section 1 | Phonics

Long Vowels

 Some words with the letter a, e, i, o, or u have long vowel sounds. They sound the same as the way you say the letters.

A. Say the things. Then write the correct long vowels.

Long Vowels 9.1

- a — cake
- e — evening
- i — kite
- o — bone
- u — flute

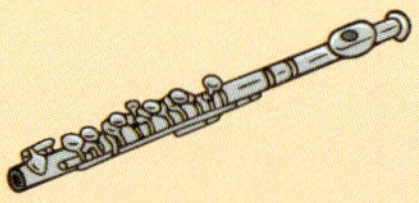

1. sm__le
2. c__ne
3. gr__pes
4. b__ke
5. __quals
6. t__be
7. pl__ne
8. c__be

38 Complete English Success (Grade 2)

B. Say the things. Then color the ones that contain the long vowel sound for each group.

Long Vowels

1.  a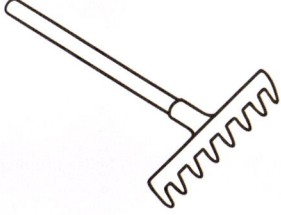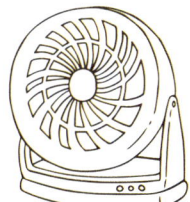

2. e

3.  i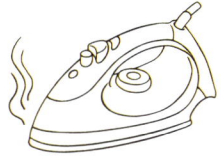

4. o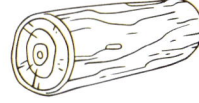

5. u

C. Say the words and circle the long vowels. Then draw lines to match the words with the pictures.

Long-vowel Words

- sp(i)der
- r(u)ler
- wh(a)le
- gl(o)be
- (a)corn
- f(i)re
- z(e)bra
- m(u)sic
- (e)vent
- (o)cean

D. **Read the passage and circle the long-vowel words with the specified colors.**

All about Plants

Most plants start as seeds. Usually, you plant the seed in the garden or the yard, in the shade or the sun.

If you use a small spade, you can dig a hole to poke the seed down and cover it with soil. Plant the seed and let the sun shine down on it. When it sprouts and the stem gets stronger, leaves begin to come out.

Long Vowels
- a — red
- o — blue
- u — green

Words That I Have Learned

Long-vowel Words

a _____

e _____

i _____

o _____

u _____

Section 1 Phonics

Y as a Vowel

 In some words, y sounds like a long "i." In some other words, y sounds like a long "e."

A. Say the words. Then write "i" or "e" in the boxes to show the sounds of "y" as a vowel.

Y as Long "i"

fly

eyes

cry

1.  spy ____

2.  cherry ____

3.  baby ____

4.  candy ____

Y as Long "e"

bunny

empty

rainy

5.  jelly ____

6.  why ____

7.  bye ____

8.  shy ____

B. Write the words in the correct boxes. Then say the words and draw lines to match.

Words with Y as a Vowel

puppy   family   fairy
July   sky   butterfly

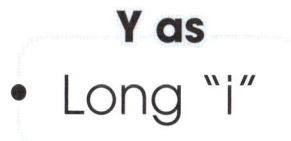
Y as Long "i"

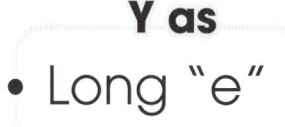
Y as Long "e"

C. **Say the words and color the boxes with the specified colors. Then fill in the blanks with the correct words.**

1. My sister's name is _____ .

2. My brother tells _____ jokes.

3. "_____" is another word for "friend."

4. Our aunt hung the clothes to _____ .

5. "If you _____ hard enough, you will win the race!" the tortoise said.

6. It was bright and _____ in the morning.

7. We can _____ our kites another day.

8. Could you come over to _____ house to play?

9. Mom is going to _____ some delicious vegetables for us to eat.

10. I have always wanted a small _____ .

D. Read the story. Then circle the words that have y with the long "i" sound and underline the words that have y with the long "e" sound.

The Coin Collection

Brittany has a coin collection. She started it when she was six years old. She put the coins in a jar labeled "My Coins."

The first coins she got were from Italy, which her mom gave her after a trip there. Since then, many of her family members have given her coins for gifts. Her dad will fly to China in July and he will try to find some special coins for her.

Brittany's favorite coin is one from Sri Lanka. It is large and heavy.

Words That I Have Learned

Y as Long "i"	Y as Long "e"
_____	_____
_____	_____
_____	_____

Complete English Success (Grade 2)

Section 1 | **Phonics**

UNIT 11 Vowel Digraphs

 A vowel digraph is two letters that, when placed together, make a single vowel sound. The letters **ai** and **ay** make the long a sound, and **ea** and **ee** make the long e sound.

A. Say the words. Then write the correct vowel digraphs.

11.1 Vowel Digraphs

Long a

ai/ay

ch**ai**n
w**ai**st

h**ay**
cl**ay**

Long e

ea/ee

l**ea**f
t**ea**ch

qu**ee**n
wh**ee**l

I love to swim in the s___ .

tr___

p___l

ch___r

I f___l so happy on my holid___ .

b___ch

B. Write the words with the "ai" and "ay" digraphs to solve the riddles.

Vowel Digraphs ai/ay

tray   snail   jay   jail   nail
say   paint   play   pay

1. You can use me to hold things together.
   _____

2. I carry my house on my back.
   _____

3. You can use me to carry things.
   _____

4. I am a blue bird.

   _____

5. You must do this if you want to buy something.

   _____

6. This is what you do when you speak.

   _____

7. You can use me to make colorful pictures.

   _____

8. You like to do this with your friends.

   _____

9. This is where people go when they commit a crime.

   _____

Section 1   Unit 11

C. Color the correct words with vowel digraphs to complete the sentences.

1. The [bee] [beat] makes its home in a hive.
2. The blue [jeans] [beans] are hanging on the line.
3. It is nice to have a cup of [tea] [tee] .
4. The baseball [team] [teem] plays in the summer.
5. The [bean] [been] plant grew very high.
6. We will have some [meat] [meet] for dinner.
7. Mom is going to [weed] [feed] the garden.
8. There are seven days in a [weak] [week] .
9. We will [see] [sea] the paintings at the art gallery.
10. This [seed] [seek] will grow into a plant.

D. Write three words for each vowel digraph.

Vowel Digraph: ea

_____

_____

_____

Vowel Digraph: ee

_____

_____

_____

E. Read the letter and circle the words with the vowel digraphs ai, ay, ea, and ee.

Adventure at the Sea

Dear Jayden,

We went to Sharaz on Thursday. On our way, we heard about a sunken ship in the deep sea. The story goes like this – a pirate ship got caught in the rain there a long time ago. It sank and a chest with precious gems and gold beads went down with it.

At first, we were afraid of the water, but then we decided to look for the ship. We boarded a small ship. Then we dived under the water. When we reached the ship, we swam inside and guess what? We found the chest!

I'll show you some photos when we're home.

Your friend,
Dean

Words That I Have Learned

Words with Vowel Digraphs

ai and ay	ea and ee
_____	_____
_____	_____
_____	_____
_____	_____

Section 1 Phonics

Section 1 Phonics

UNIT 12 Vowel Digraph: oo

 A vowel digraph is two letters that, when placed together, make a single sound. The letters **oo** can have the long oo sound, like in "room," or the short oo sound, like in "cook."

A. Say the words. Then color the pictures with the specified colors.

12.1 Vowel Digraphs

Long oo
- sp**oo**n
- t**oo**thbrush

Short oo
- w**oo**d
- b**oo**k

Long oo  (blue) **Short oo** (green)

1. h**oo**k
2. ball**oo**n
3. w**oo**l
4. l**oo**p
5. m**oo**n
6. m**oo**se
7. c**oo**k

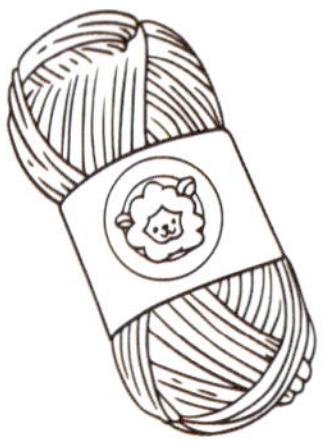

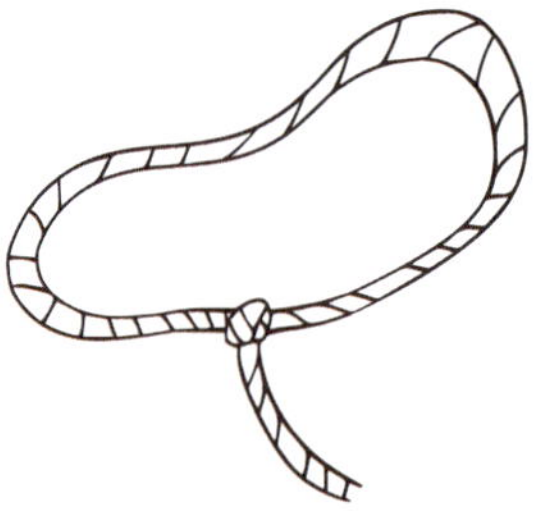

B. Write the words in the correct boxes. Then give two more examples for each vowel digraph.

Long oo	Short oo
My Examples	My Examples
_____	_____
_____	_____

Section 1   Unit 12

C. Write "long" or "short" to identify the vowel digraph of each group of words. Then fill in the blanks with the words.

1.
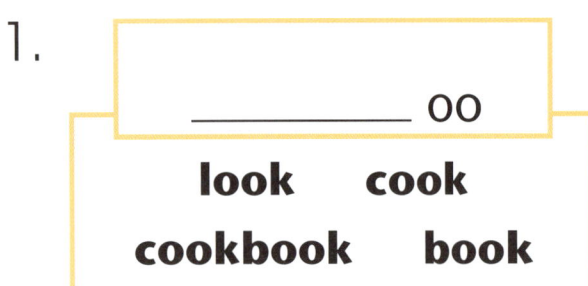
_____ oo

look   cook
cookbook   book

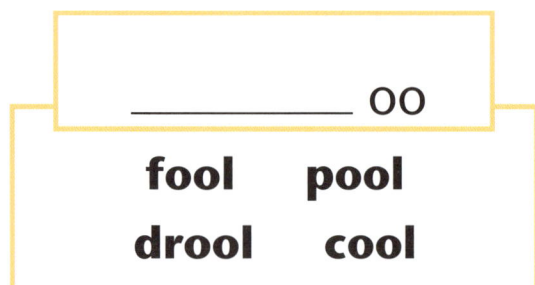
_____ oo

fool   pool
drool   cool

2.

My mom taught me to _____

By reading a _____ .

She said, "Take a _____ .

This is called a _____ ."

3.

The clown played the _____ ,

Jumping in the _____ .

He thought it was _____

When he started to _____ .

D. Read the story. Then underline and circle the words as specified.

Noor's Smoothie Recipe

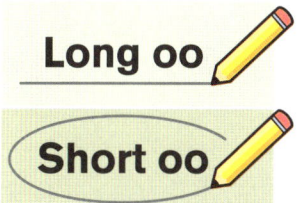

Noor was a very good cook. But she did not want to make the same food every day. So she stood in the kitchen and looked around. Finally, she decided to put some apples, strawberries, bananas, and three scoops of chocolate ice cream into the blender. She pushed the red button and "whoosh" it went as it shook the small wooden table. She excitedly poured the mixture into her glass. Noor hummed in a good mood as she drank the delicious smoothie.

Words That I Have Learned

Vowel Digraphs

Long oo

_____

_____

_____

Short oo

_____

_____

_____

Section 1 Phonics

Diphthongs

 A diphthong is a vowel sound in a single syllable that begins with the sound of one vowel and ends with the sound of another vowel.

A. Say the things. Then write the correct diphthongs.

Diphthongs

ou — couch

ow — owl

oi — oil

oy — boy

1. bl____se

2. c____l

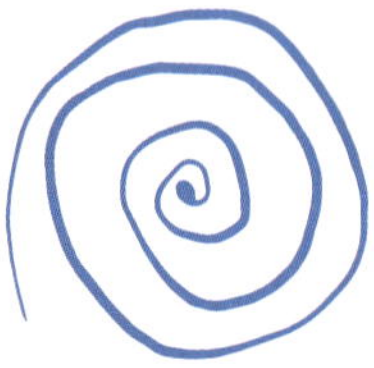

3. m____se

4. cr____n

5. ____ster

6. t____

7. p____son

8. fr____n

54   Complete English Success (Grade 2)

B. Say the words in each group and label the box with the correct diphthong. Then fill in the blank with the correct word.

Diphthongs

ou   ow   oi   oy

1. ☐ **destroy   royal   enjoy   annoy**

The _____ castle was very beautiful.

2. ☐ **soil   choice   moist   noise**

Stephanie heard a loud _____ when the balloon popped.

3. ☐ **howl   drown   town   gown**

The people of the small _____ celebrated the mayor's birthday.

4. ☐ **loud   round   south   mouth**

Johnny opened his _____ to show his cavity to the dentist.

Complete English Success (Grade 2)

C. Say the words. Then write them in the correct boxes.

Diphthongs

ou	ow	oi	oy

D. Read the story. Then circle the diphthongs ou, ow, oi, and oy.

Roy the Toy Robot

Roy was very annoyed with his sister, Joy. She was around two years old and enjoyed destroying his things. She even spoiled his favorite drawing of blue clouds over a sea of trout and the one with a crowd of silly clowns. At first, Roy yelled at her in a loud voice. Then he heard her cry on the couch. So he decided to surprise her. He took a piece of foil, some brown paper, and a metal coil. After a lot of hard work, "Roy the Toy Robot" went to his sister and they played together until their mother was back home.

Words That I Have Learned

Words with Diphthongs

ou _____

ow _____

oi _____

oy _____

Section 1 | Phonics

Rhyming Words

 Rhyming words are words that have the same ending sound.

A. Say the things. Then color each rhyming pair with the same color.

Rhyming Words	
b**one**	
c**one**	
k**ite**	
l**ight**	
p**in**	
b**in**	
c**at**	
m**at**	

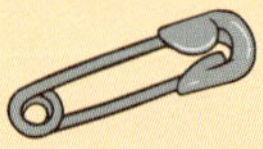

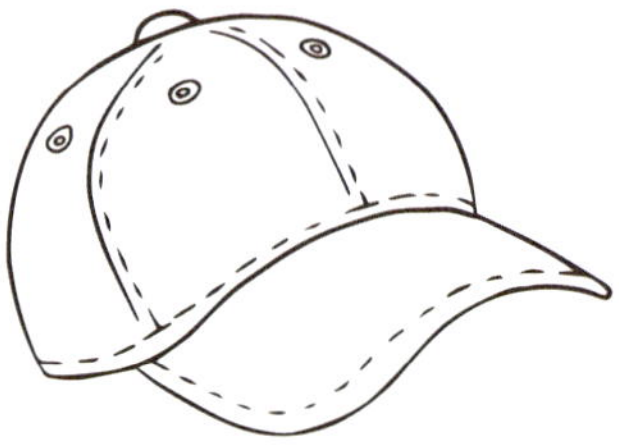

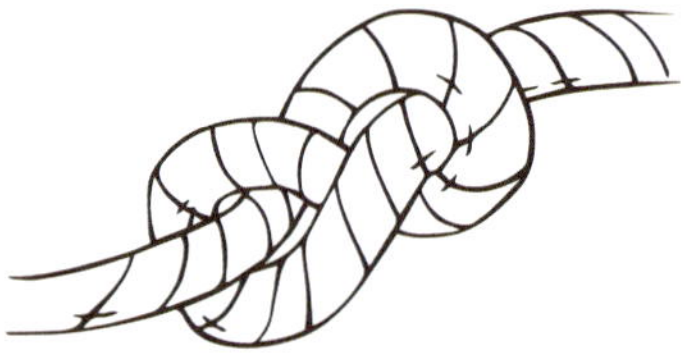

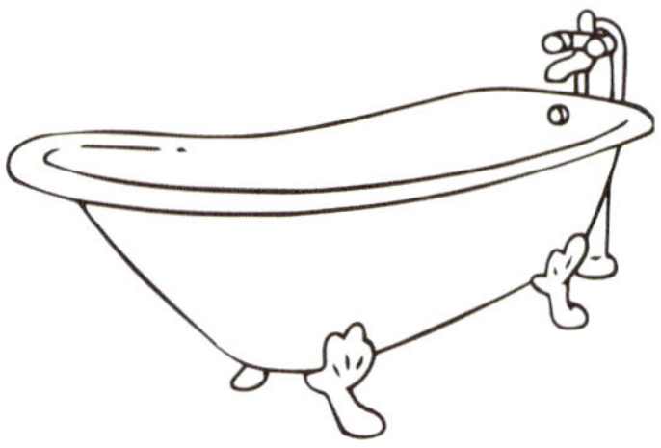

B. Name each item. Then cross out the word that does not rhyme in each group.

1.

door
hook
look
cook

2.

luck
truck
quack
stuck

3.

lake
cage
bake
make

4.

wok
dog
log
fog

5.

run
one
bun
mom

6.

man
train
cane
stain

Section 1   Unit 14

C. **Complete the crossword puzzle with words that rhyme with the clues.**

 Rhyming words do not have to end with the same spelling.

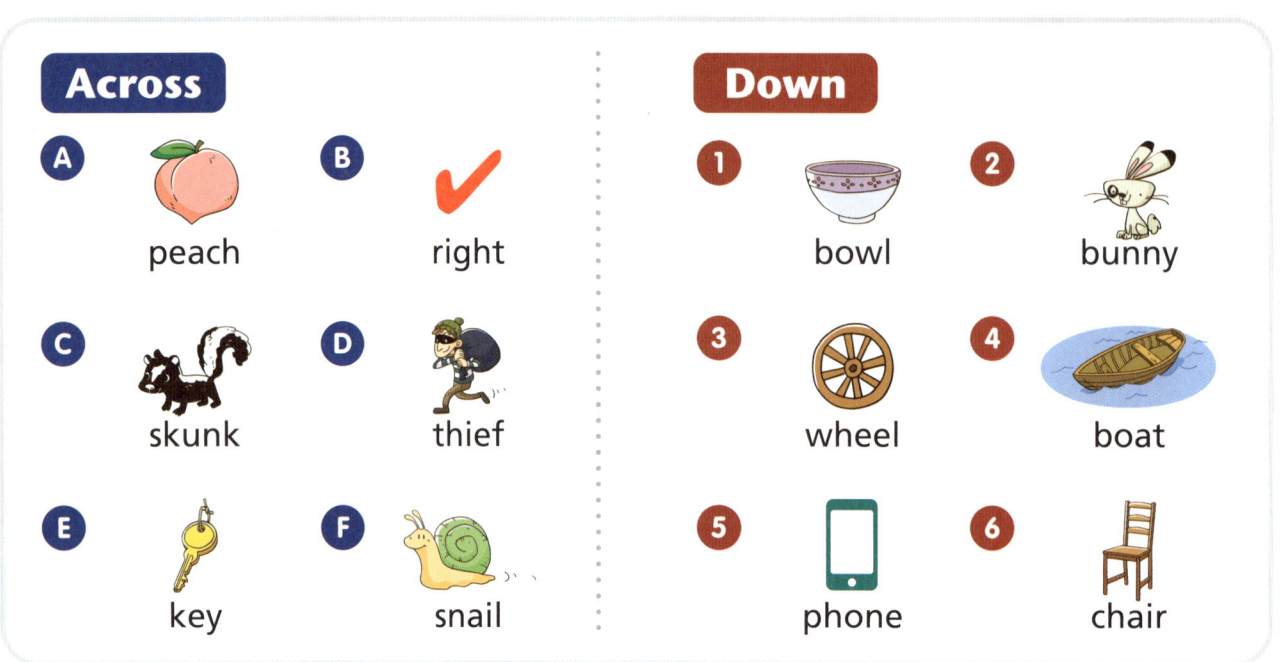

D. Circle each pair or group of rhyming words with the same color.

Deep in the Woods

In the woods so deep,
I see a little white sheep,
A cat chasing a rat,
And a bear and a hare
Sharing a big juicy pear!
At the pond I can hear
A dog barking at a frog
And a moose grunting at a goose!
In the woods so deep,
I drift off to sleep.

Words That I Have Learned

Rhyming Words

_____

_____

_____

_____

Review 1 — Phonics

A. **Circle the answers.**

1. The _____ consonant of the picture is "L."

   beginning

   middle

   ending

2. Which one has the hard "c" sound?

3. Which word contains the silent "k"?

   kite

   knife

   kitten

4. Which blend does this picture have?

   bl

   cl

   pl

5. Which one has an R blend?

   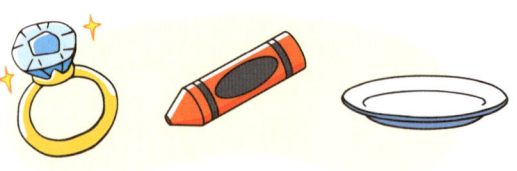

6. This picture has the _____ blend.

   L

   R

   S

7. Which group contains all words that have consonant digraphs?

   wheel, thumb, chair

   thumb, crown, chair

   shampoo, frog, knee

8. This picture has a _____ sound.

   short vowel

   long vowel

   diphthong

9. This picture has the ____ sound.

    short "a"

    long "a"

    vowel digraph "ay"

10. Which picture has y with the long "i" sound?

11. This picture has the vowel digraph "____."

    ai

    ay

    ee

12. Which word has the short "oo" sound?

    moon

    spoon

    hook

13. Which one does not have a diphthong?

14. The word "avoid" has a ____.

    digraph

    long vowel

    diphthong

15. Which pair of words rhyme?

    pin, been

    bite, sight

    cone, come

16. Which one does not rhyme with the others?

Review 1 — Phonics

Consonants

B. Say the things. Then draw lines to match.

- middle consonant "m"
- ending consonant "l"
- silent consonant "b"
- silent consonant "h"

C. Read the sentences. Then circle the letters with the specified colors.

1. The gigantic giant, Gary, used magic to decorate the castle.
2. There were cakes and candies in the garden on Carl's birthday.
3. The dancers celebrated as Andy played the guitar.

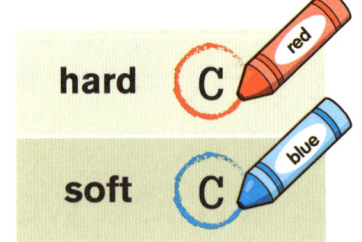
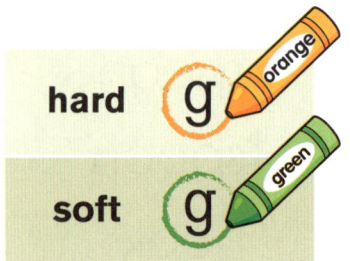

Consonant Blends and Digraphs

D. Say the things. Then write the correct consonant blends.

1. __ __ock
2. __ __um
3. __ __ar
4. __ __ies
5. __ __irt
6. __ __ag

E. Cross out the picture that does not belong in each group.

Consonant Digraphs

1. ch
2. sh
3. th
4. wh

Review 1 — Phonics

Short and Long Vowels

F. Say the things. Write the correct short and long vowels in the circles. Then give three more examples for each.

G. Read the sentences. Then write the underlined words in the correct columns.

	Short-vowel Word	Long-vowel Word
1. <u>Bill</u> likes <u>grapes</u>.	_____	_____
2. They bought a <u>pink</u> <u>slide</u>.	_____	_____
3. He left a beautiful <u>rose</u> on the front <u>mat</u>.	_____	_____
4. Beatrice's <u>pet</u> dog ran away with the <u>bone</u>.	_____	_____
5. Jameson spent the <u>night</u> collecting <u>rocks</u>.	_____	_____

Complete English Success (Grade 2)

Vowel Digraphs and Diphthongs

H. Fill in the blanks with the correct vowel digraphs using the picture clues.

1. The qu___n took a rest under the tr___ .

2. I saw a little sn___l on a l___f.

3. Dad hammered a n___l into the tr___ .

4. The red ball___n flew up to the m___n.

I. Read the sentences. Then write the underlined words in the correct boxes.

1. The sun shone through the <u>clouds</u> as the children played <u>outside</u>.

2. Alia colored the <u>crown</u> with a yellow crayon and used a <u>brown</u> one for the <u>soil</u>.

3. The little <u>boy</u> heard an <u>annoying</u> <u>noise</u> so he went to investigate.

Words with the Diphthongs:

ou	ow	oi	oy
_____	_____	_____	_____
_____	_____	_____	_____

Complete English Success (Grade 2)

Section 2
Grammar

 Scan this QR code or go to Download Center at **www.popularbookusa.com** to watch our fun videos on grammar!

 Pronouns

 Verbs

 Subject-verb Agreement

 Prepositions

 Types of Sentences

 What is a Contraction?

Section 2 | Grammar

Nouns

 A **common noun** names any person, animal, place, or thing.

A **proper noun** names a specific person, animal, place, or thing. It always begins with a capital letter.

Examples

Common Noun		Proper Noun
girl		Ana
dog		Poodle
city		Houston
movie		Bambi

A. Write the nouns in the correct places. Begin the proper nouns with capital letters.

> frisbee   city   seattle   game
> dalmatian   boy   dog   timmy

	Common Noun		Proper Noun
Person	_____		_____
Animal	_____		_____
Place	_____		_____
Thing	_____		_____

A **singular noun** names one person, animal, place, or thing. A **plural noun** names more than one person, animal, place, or thing.

Many plural nouns are formed by adding "s" to the singular nouns.

For nouns ending in "s," "x," "ch," or "sh," add "es" to form the plural.

For nouns ending in "y," change "y" to "i" and add "es."

Examples

Singular Noun	Plural Noun
girl	girls
bus	buses
box	boxes
beach	beaches
dish	dishes
berry	berries

B. Circle the correct words.

1.
parrot / parrots

2.
fairy / fairies

3.
foxs / foxes

4.
dress / dresses

5.
brush / brushes

6.
chicks / chickes

7.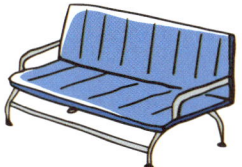
bench / benches

8.
rat / rats

9.
kids / kides

Section 2   Unit 1

Some nouns are **countable**. You can use number words before their plural forms.

Some nouns are **uncountable**. You cannot use number words before them and they do not have any plural forms.

Examples

- There are five <u>apples</u> in the basket. ↑ countable

- <u>Milk</u> is good for us. ↑ uncountable

C. Look at each picture. If it is countable, draw to show more than one and add "s/es" to make the noun plural.

carrot___   jam___   popcorn___

glass___   ball___   cheese___

D. Color the correct nouns for the sentences.

1. Pour some [water] [waters] into the two [cup] [cups].

2. The [bottle] [bottles] are made of [plastic] [plastics].

3. Add some [sand] [sands] to these [pot] [pots].

4. I have [faith] [faiths] in both [hero] [heroes].

Complete English Success (Grade 2)

E. Read the story and write the underlined words in the correct boxes.

Arnie's Farm

Arnie's <u>farm</u> is far from the <u>market</u>. Every day, Arnie works very hard. He turns the <u>soil</u>, which is sometimes called <u>dirt</u>, to make it easier to retain <u>air</u> and drain <u>water</u>. He milks the <u>cows</u> and takes care of other <u>animals</u>. There are <u>hens</u> that lay <u>eggs</u> and <u>sheep</u> that provide <u>wool</u>. Every Saturday, Arnie drives to the market to sell the eggs, <u>milk</u>, and wool.

Countable Noun

Uncountable Noun

Words That I Have Learned

Nouns

_____

_____

_____

Section 2 | Grammar

UNIT 2 Articles

"A," "an," and "the" are **articles**. They come before nouns. "A" is used before a noun that begins with a consonant sound. "An" is used before a noun that begins with a vowel sound. "The" is used before a noun that names a particular person, place, or thing. It is also used with something unique.

Examples
- <u>a</u> girl
- <u>an</u> honor
- <u>the</u> Bahamas
- <u>the</u> moon

A. Put the words in the correct boxes. Then give one more example for each.

apricot

South Pole

house

umbrella

idea

uniform

White House

NYPD

album

violin

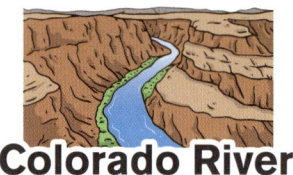
Colorado River

Articles

a	an	the
_____	_____	_____
my example	my example	my example

B. Write what each picture is with the correct article.

a/an/the

unicorn   moon   owl   sun   airplane
North Pole   elephant   rainbow   lamp

1.
_____

2.
_____

3.
_____

4.
a. _____
b. _____

5.
_____

6.
_____

7.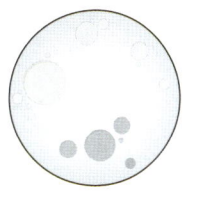
_____

8.
_____

C. Circle the correct articles to complete the sentences.

1. Do you know **an / the** girl over there?

2. Is this **a / an** orange or **a / the** grapefruit?

3. There are no penguins at **a / the** North Pole. You can only find them at **a / the** South Pole.

4. **An / The** Rockies are a mountain range in North America.

5. Look at **a / the** ape in **a / the** book. Is it **a / an** chimpanzee?

6. We have forgotten to buy one of **an / the** ingredients. We need **an / the** avocado.

7. **A / The** friend should be one who cares about your feelings.

8. The train left **a / an** hour ago.

9. There is **a / the** library on **an / the** eighth floor.

10. I wish I could fly in **a / the** sky.

An article can be used before a noun with an adjective. Use "a" if the adjective begins with a consonant sound. Use "an" if it begins with a vowel sound. Use "the" if the noun after the adjective refers to a particular person, place, or thing.

Examples
- a beautiful flower
- an honest girl
- the national anthem

D. Write a sentence with the adjective and the noun. Use the correct article before them.

1. oval table

   _____

2. Great Lakes

   _____

3. American flag

   _____

4. kind person

   _____

Words That I Have Learned

Articles

a   _____

an _____

the _____

Section 2 | Grammar

Pronouns

 A **pronoun** replaces a noun. A **subject pronoun** acts as the subject in a sentence.

"I," "you," "we," "he," "she," "it," and "they" are subject pronouns.

Example

Kim is my classmate. He is my neighbor too.

Kim

A. Draw lines to match the words and the picture with the correct subject pronouns.

The squirrel •

Ray and I •

Cindy •

The acorn •

Mr. Hopkins •

You and Liam •

Alexa and Ezra •

The flowers •

•

Subject Pronouns

• I

• You

• We

• He

• She

• It

• They

B. **Circle the correct subject pronouns to complete the sentences.**

1. **We / It** went to the movies last night.

2. **They / She** both like skiing.

3. Melissa likes collecting coins. **You / She** keeps them in a big jar.

4. My family and I are visiting Niagara Falls this summer. **He / It** is in New York State.

5. **I / You** don't know where the restaurant is. Could you show me the way?

C. **Replace the underlined words with subject pronouns. Write above the words.**

<u>Mom and Dad</u> take my brother and me to the zoo. <u>My family and I</u> go to see the zebras first. <u>My brother Cecil</u> takes pictures of the zebras. <u>One of the zebras</u> looks at us.

Section 2   Unit 3

An **object pronoun** receives the action of the verb in a sentence.

"Me," "you," "us," "him," "her," "it," and "them" are object pronouns.

Example

Mrs. Lin drives Leo to school.
Mrs. Lin drives him to school.

D. Circle the object pronouns in the sentences.

1. I will meet you at the mall entrance.
2. Your ice cream is melting. Finish it quickly.
3. There were two mice in the corner, but no one noticed them except me!
4. Janice gave him a call when she arrived at the airport.
5. Miss Hall has given us two choices for the outing. We have to let her know our pick tomorrow.

E. Write the correct object pronouns for the words.

1. my sister   _____
2. Mr. and Mrs. Hall   _____
3. our class   _____
4. you and Ella   _____
5. the actor   _____
6. Lily and me   _____
7. his tall hat   _____

8. _____

Kevin the Clown

Mia and her cat

F. **Fill in the blanks with the correct object pronouns to complete the sentences.**

1. Mom took this photo of _____ on the farm.

2. Ginny has a dog. She walks _____ in the park every day.

3. Hilda and Jon are my best friends. I will surely invite _____ to my party.

4. Dennis is very upset. Do you know what happened to _____ ?

5. Mr. Soto promised to tell _____ the story ending tomorrow. We cannot wait to know how the story goes.

6. Ana is sick. Mom is giving _____ some medicine.

Words That I Have Learned

Subject Pronoun	Object Pronoun
_____	_____
_____	_____
_____	_____
_____	_____

Section 2 Grammar

UNIT 4 Present Tense Verbs

A **present tense verb** tells what happens now. Add "s" to the base form of the verb to tell about one person or thing, except "I" and "you."

Use the "ing" form of the verb with "am/is/are" to tell what someone or something is doing.

Examples
- I <u>live</u> in Texas.
- My aunt <u>lives</u> in Denver.
- The children <u>are reading</u>.

A. Complete the chart.

	Base Form	"s" Form	"ing" Form
1.		sings	
2.	laugh		
3.		breaks	
4.			leaping
5.	snow		
6.		finds	

B. **Write the correct forms of the underlined verbs above them.**

1. The sun <u>shine</u> brightly.

2. The children are <u>walks</u> along the pond.

3. They <u>chats</u> happily.

4. Some ducks <u>lives</u> in the pond.

5. Derek is <u>waves</u> at the ducks.

6. The ducks are <u>look</u> at Derek.

C. **Fill in the blanks with the verbs in the correct forms.**

| stay | get | play | eat | collect | blow |

1. I _____ toast for breakfast every day.

2. It _____ dark after the sun sets.

3. We _____ in the tent at night.

4. The wind is _____ fiercely.

5. Jerry _____ hockey on the weekends.

6. The bees are _____ nectar.

Section 2 **Unit 4**

"**Am**," "**is**," and "**are**" are the present forms of the verb "be."

Use "am" with "I." Use "is" to tell about one person, animal, place, or thing. Use "are" to tell about more than one person, animal, place, or thing.

Examples
- I <u>am</u> a student.
- Mom's cake <u>is</u> yummy.
- Pandas <u>are</u> black and white.

D. Circle the correct forms of "be" to complete the sentences.

1. Bees **am / is / are** busy insects.

2. The flowers **am / is / are** in full bloom.

3. That **am / is / are** a big flower!

4. Nectar **am / is / are** my favorite treat.

5. The nectar of the flowers **am / is / are** sweet.

6. Where **am / is / are** the other bees?

7. There **am / is / are** more flowers over there!

8.
   How **am / is / are** you?

   I **am / is / are** exhausted!

Remember that "am," "is," and "are" can be used with the "ing" form of verbs to tell what someone or something is doing.

Examples
- I <u>am watching</u> TV.
- He <u>is having</u> a good time.
- They <u>are making</u> a kite.

E. **Look at each picture and put the words in order to write about what is happening.**

A

B

C

reading   am   I
letter.   a

happily.   the   are
calves   playing

is   in   tree.   the
swinging   Gavin

A _____

B _____

C _____

That I Have Learned

Present Tense Verbs

_____

_____

_____

Section 2 Grammar

Past Tense Verbs

 A **past tense verb** tells about something that happened in the past. For most verbs, add "d" or "ed" to the base form to change them to the past form.

Examples

Base Form	Past Form
use	used
fold	folded

A. Circle the past forms of the verbs in the word search.

close   score   lift
brush   erase   reach
dislike buzz   collect

c	e	p	d	r	h	l	c	o	l	r	f	a
o		l	i	t	e	b	u	z	z	e	d	
b	a	d	s	g	e	r	a	s	l	a	e	t
r	s	h	l	r	t	u	r	o	i	c	b	e
c	l	o	s	e	d	s	e	r	f	h	u	r
o	j	u	c	a	m	h	a	i	t	e	z	a
l		c	o	l	l	e	c	t	e	d	s	s
e	p	b	r	u	s	d	d	b	d		c	e
c	o	r	e	a	d		k	m	c	e	o	d
d	q	t	d	i	s	l	i	k	e	d	s	g

Some past tense verbs are formed by repeating the last letter before adding "ed."

For verbs ending in "y," change "y" to "i" before adding "ed."

Examples

Base Form	Past Form
slip	slipped
study	studied

B. Circle the correct past forms of the verbs to complete the story.

Dodo **carryed / carried** a backpack to school yesterday. He **learnd / learned** some funny tricks at the dog school. He **balanced / balanceed** himself with one hand on a plank on a ball. After that, he **skiped / skipped** for an hour. Then he **hurryed / hurried** home for lunch. On his way home, he **remembered / rememberred** that there was no more dog food at home, so he **stoped / stopped** by a grocery store and **grabed / grabbed** some dog food. He also **tryed / tried** to look for a bone as a treat, but he could not find one that he **liked / likeed** .

Section 2   Unit 5

 Irregular past tense verbs do not end in "ed." They may be spelled the same as the base form or they may be completely different.

Examples

Base Form	Past Form
put	put
go	went

C. Write the past forms of the verbs.

1.

stand

_____

2.

catch

_____

3.

burst

_____

4.

buy

_____

5.

weep

_____

6.

throw

_____

7.

teach

_____

8.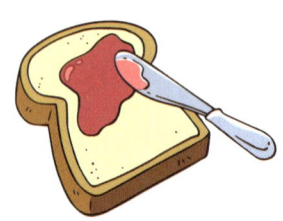

spread

_____

"**Was**" and "**were**" are the past forms of the verb "be."

Use "was" to tell about one person, animal, place, or thing. Use "were" to tell about more than one person, animal, place, or thing.

"Was" and "were" can also be used with the "ing" form of a verb to tell what someone or something was doing at a past time.

Examples

- There <u>was</u> a storm last night.
- The kittens <u>were</u> frightened.
- They <u>were shaking</u> with fear.

D. Check if the underlined words are correct. Correct the wrong ones by writing above them.

1. It <u>were</u> raining when he walked his dog.

2. There <u>was</u> a bird in the tree this morning.

3. The kids <u>were</u> singing when the teacher came in.

4. Hilary and I <u>was</u> at the show last night.

Words That I Have Learned

Past Tense Verbs

_____

_____

_____

Section 2 | Grammar

Adjectives

An **adjective** tells about a noun. It describes a person, an animal, a place, or a thing. Color words, number words, and shape words are all adjectives.

Examples
- The <u>little</u> girl is <u>skinny</u>.
- Bananas are <u>yellow</u>.
- There are <u>three</u> apples on a <u>square</u> plate.

A. Look at the pictures. Then draw lines to match the adjectives with the correct nouns.

Adjectives

- three
- naughty
- beautiful
- tall
- freezing
- angry

B. Read each group of adjectives and write the noun they describe to solve the riddle.

> candy   castle   ball   cat   diamond
> tree   apple   sweater   girl   book

juicy
round
red

soft
cuddly
cute

shiny
clear
hard

1. _____   2. _____   3. _____

warm
cozy
soft

sweet
hard
colorful

interesting
heavy
big

4. _____   5. _____   6. _____

green
strong
tall

pretty
kind
cheerful

7. _____   8. _____

royal
old
haunted

bouncy
round
big

9. _____   10. _____

Section 2 **Unit 6**

C. Unscramble the words and fill in the blanks with the correct adjectives.

1. _____ apples are usually sour.
   ereGn

2. I want a _____ peach after dinner.
   yicju

3. A rainbow has _____ colors.
   eesnv

4. Mom wants to buy a _____ table.
   norud

5. My brother likes eating _____ curry.
   pcsyi

6. Do you see my _____ yo-yo? I just bought it
   enw
   yesterday. It has a _____ star in the middle.
   oelwyl

7. Pandas are _____ and _____ in color.
   lakcb   hewit
   They eat only _____ bamboo shoots.
   sherf

8. Sam looks _____. He does not understand
   zuzpeld
   what Jake is doing.

9. It is such a _____ pig.
   yazl
   It is always sleeping.

D. **Circle the adjectives in the sentences. Then rewrite the sentences by replacing the adjectives with other adjectives.**

1. Uncle Rowan caught a big fish yesterday.

   _____

   _____

2. She looks pretty in that costume.

   _____

3. The dog has just given birth to six puppies.

   _____

4. I dreamed of a scary monster last night.

   _____

5. The red roses in the yard were a gift from Nova.

   _____

Words That I Have Learned

Adjectives

_____

_____

_____

Section 2 | Grammar

Prepositions

 Prepositions of place are location words. They tell where people, animals, or things are.

Examples
Pete is <u>in</u> his pet shop. He is putting the paper <u>on</u> the board.

A. Circle the correct prepositions of place to complete the sentences.

1. There are lots of stars **in / on** the night sky.

2. The shy girl hides **between / behind** her mom.

3. Did you see that dog jump **under / over** the fence?

4. Please leave the books **on / over** the table **in / by** the window.

5. There is a bakery **in / between** the grocery store and the Italian restaurant.

6. Ken is already waiting **under / at** the bus stop.

   We spent too much time **in / beside** the toy store just then.

B. **Look at the picture and read the story. Check the circles if the underlined prepositions of place are correct. If not, write the correct prepositions above the words.**

Samuel is under ◯ a cruise ship. He is sitting at ◯ a table in ◯ the deck enjoying the cool breeze. There are some clouds over ◯ the sky, but the weather is still fine. There is a drink under ◯ the table. Samuel does not know what is in ◯ the glass, but he thinks it tastes amazing. A little bird is in front of ◯ Samuel. It seems to want to share the tranquil moment with him. The cruise ship is not too far on ◯ the shore. Samuel can see people that look as tiny as ants between ◯ the beach.

Section 2 **Unit 7**

 Prepositions of time are used with other words to tell when someone does something or when something happens.

Examples
- We go to the park every day <u>in</u> the summer.
- The sun is high up in the sky <u>at</u> noon.

C. Fill in the blanks with the correct prepositions of time.

Prepositions of Time
in   on   at

1. Let's go to the movies _____ Friday night.

2. The flowers bloom _____ the spring.

3. The baseball game starts _____ eight o'clock tonight.

4. We are planning a trip to Germany _____ November.

5. What are you going to dress up as _____ Halloween?

6. Dad and his friends meet _____ the first day of every month.

7. Why don't we talk about this _____ lunchtime?

8. We like going to the beach _____ weekends.

D. Read the passage and circle the underlined prepositions with the specified colors.

Disney World

Disney World is an adventure park <u>in</u> Orlando, Florida. There are many Disney characters <u>in</u> the park. You can also see them <u>in</u> different parades that happen <u>at</u> different times <u>during</u> the day.

Disney World is an exciting place to visit. You can go there early <u>in</u> the morning and enjoy the whole day there. You can go on the many rides <u>around</u> the park. You can also try different types of foods <u>in</u> a variety of restaurants and <u>at</u> food kiosks. One of the most special moments to enjoy is the spectacular fireworks show that happens every day <u>at</u> sundown.

Disney World is known as the happiest place <u>on</u> Earth! Why not go there <u>on</u> a weekend or <u>in</u> the summer and enjoy the place where dreams come true?

Words That I Have Learned

Preposition of Place

_____

_____

_____

Preposition of Time

_____

_____

_____

Section 2 Grammar

UNIT 8 Joining Words

Joining words connect ideas in sentences.

"And" adds information or lists ideas.

"Or" lists options.

"But" joins contrasting ideas.

Examples
- Let's sing <u>and</u> dance.
- Do you want hot <u>or</u> cold tea?
- That rabbit is small <u>but</u> fast.

A. Circle the joining words in the sentences.

1. Emi, Zoe, and Jon had great fun at Brad's birthday party.

2. This machine is old, but it still works well.

3. Green and purple are my favorite colors.

4. Is Rome or Venice the capital of Italy?

5. Pick one flavor combination: strawberry and banana or mango and coconut.

6. Nobody but Julian could solve the puzzle.

7. Will it be sunny or rainy tomorrow?

8. The pink candies are sweet, but the yellow and green ones are sour.

9. Adalyn wanted to try the berry pie, but she was already too full.

B. **Fill in the blanks with the correct joining words.**

Joining Words
and   or   but

1. A hat _____ a cap will protect you from the sun.

2. Jam _____ butter taste so good together.

3. The teacher gave us two days to study, _____ it was not enough.

4. I like soccer, _____ it is very hard to play.

5. Susie _____ her sister wanted to visit either the museum _____ the aquarium. They did not have time for both. _____ on the day they decided to go, they had guests over _____ they played cards with them instead.

Section 2 **Unit 8**

C. Check if the joining word in each sentence is correct. If not, cross it out and write the correct joining word above it.

1. I want to be a doctor, a lawyer, or an actor.

2. Do you want to be a chef or work in a restaurant?

3. Mom works very hard, but she likes her job.

4. I have to practice hard but be better at dancing.

5. My brother only has one day off in a week. It is Saturday and Sunday.

D. Join the two sentences with "and," "or," or "but."

1. My sister brushed her hair. She put on her favorite dress.
   _____
   _____

2. I wanted to show my picture to you. It got ruined in the rain.
   _____
   _____

3. Rehearse more. You will not remember the lines.
   _____
   _____

E. Read the story and add joining words wherever needed.

Playing Soccer

Today I started soccer. My twin brother, Michael, ^*and* I went to a big field. There were lots of children, none were beginners like us. Some of them were practicing their skills others were playing a game.

The coach told us to pick an orange uniform a green one. I liked the green uniform, Michael liked the orange one.

Our coach was very nice friendly. She told us that we would practice once a week, either on Saturday Sunday. She said that the most important thing was to have fun.

Words That I Have Learned

Joining Words

_____

_____

_____

Other Words

_____

_____

_____

Section 2 | Grammar

UNIT 9 The Sentence: Subject and Predicate

A **sentence** tells a complete thought about someone or something. It begins with a capital letter and ends with a period (.).

Example

The children are having fun.

A. Check the correct boxes to show what is missing from the sentences.

Missing

	Capital Letter	Period
1. The monkeys are playing in the tree	☐	☐
2. there is a bridge over there	☐	☐
3. I want a cup of tea	☐	☐
4. the dog is hungry.	☐	☐
5. the baby is crying loudly	☐	☐
6. she never likes wearing a cap.	☐	☐
7. my grandma makes yummy muffins.	☐	☐
8. we play badminton after school	☐	☐
9. The musical fountain is in the center of the mall	☐	☐

A sentence has two main parts – a subject and a predicate.

The **subject** tells whom or what the sentence is about.

Example

Jerry is looking at the ant.

B. Circle the correct subjects for the sentences.

1. **The baby / Mrs. Maddison** holds a party for Brad's birthday.

2. **Brad's father / Brad's cat** puts six candles on the cake.

3. **The birthday cake / The candles** is big.

4. **Andy / Nina** has a flower on her T-shirt.

5. **The children / The cups** are wearing party hats.

6. **Brad's parents / Brad** give him a bike for a present.

7. **The party hats / The children** play games.

8. **They / It** have great fun at the party.

9. **Mrs. Maddison / Brad** is making a wish.

10. **Andy / The bike** is telling Zoe to be quiet.

11. **The birthday / The party** ends around five.

Complete English Success (Grade 2)

Section 2 — Unit 9

 The **predicate** is the part of a sentence that tells what the subject is or what the subject does.

Example
The dog likes playing with a ball.

C. Complete the sentences with the correct predicates. Write the letters.

1. My brother _____ .
2. You _____ .
3. The shops _____ .
4. My cat _____ .
5. The bus stop _____ .
6. The book _____ .
7. The Statue of Liberty _____ .
8. The mother bird _____ .

Predicates

- **A** is newly added to this route
- **B** are closed on New Year's Day
- **C** looks like a tiger
- **D** is located in New York
- **E** is working on his Science project
- **F** need a stick to play hockey
- **G** is about animals of the jungle
- **H** is feeding her babies in the nest

Complete English Success (Grade 2)

D. **Look at the picture. Then complete the sentences with subjects or predicates.**

1. _____ are at a campsite.
2. _____ sees a raccoon.
3. _____ are floating in the sky.
4. The children _____ .
5. The raccoon _____ .
6. A bear _____ .

Words That I Have Learned

_____

_____

_____

Section 2 | Grammar

UNIT 10 Subjects and Objects

The **subject** of a verb is the person or thing that performs the action. It can be a noun with its modifiers, or a pronoun.

Examples
- The little boy played the piano.
- He also played the violin.

A. Underline the subject of the verb in each sentence.

1. The girl is pointing at the bird.
2. The hungry lion is chasing the antelope.
3. The hamburger on the plate looks yummy.
4. My mom and dad went to the same high school.
5. The book on the shelf belongs to Heidi.
6. She has left her lunch bag in the kitchen.
7. Ted and his sister like playing board games together.
8. The cute kitten is trying to catch the butterfly.
9. That boy over there won the race last year.
10. Kayla, Miles, and I will work on the project tonight.
11. The busy beaver is building a dam.

The **object** of a verb is the person or thing that receives the action. Like a subject, it can be a noun with its modifiers, or a pronoun.

Examples
- Noah is feeding his pet turtles.
- He feeds them every morning.

B. **Underline the object of the verb if there is one in the sentence. If not, put a cross in the circle.**

1. Lillian likes all flavors of ice cream.
2. The naughty cat broke the vase by the window.
3. We have to leave early tomorrow morning.
4. Chris baked an apple pie.
5. Luke wore a warm jacket yesterday.
6. Sofia played computer games after dinner.
7. Everyone played, sang, and danced happily.
8. Daniel wakes up at seven o'clock every day.
9. My dad finished all the soup in the big bowl.
10. Please remind Samuel and me again tomorrow.

Section 2 **Unit 10**

C. Put the words in order to write the subjects and the objects of the verbs. Then write "S" in the boxes if they are subjects and "O" if they are objects.

Allen the Chipmunk

1. _____ ☐ lives in
   Chipmunk Allen the

the forest with his family.

2. _____ ☐ provide
   trees the in forest The

3. _____ ☐ for them.
   and food shelter

Allen loves 4. _____ ☐. He also likes
              nuts seeds and

5. _____ ☐. He can very easily and
   fruit fresh

quickly climb 6. _____ ☐. He likes playing
                 trees tall

7. _____ ☐ with his friends in the trees
   fun various games

every day. 8. _____ ☐ always remind
              parents Their

9. _____ ☐ to be careful outside, so
   and Allen friends his

they would warn 10. _____ ☐ of danger
                    another one

whenever they play out there in the forest. They

make 11. _____ ☐ to do this.
         sounds different

D. Write sentences of your own using each word as the subject of a verb in one sentence and as the object in another sentence.

Flowers are beautiful.
  subject

I love flowers.
  object

flowers

sun

Subject: _____

Object: _____

photos

Subject: _____

Object: _____

children

Subject: _____

Object: _____

Words That I Have Learned

_____
_____
_____

Complete English Success (Grade 2)

Section 2 | Grammar

UNIT 11 Types of Sentences

A **telling sentence** tells about someone or something. It ends with a period (.).

An **asking sentence** asks about someone or something. It ends with a question mark (?).

Examples

Telling Sentence

A bicycle has two wheels.

Asking Sentence

How many wheels does a tricycle have?

A. Read the sentences and put the correct punctuation marks in the circles. Then write the letters in the correct boxes.

A Plants need sunlight and water ◯

B There are lots of flowers in the garden ◯

C What do you want for dinner ◯

D This is an ice-cream parlor ◯

E What's that in your hand ◯

F Is that what you want ◯

G Isn't it amazing ◯

H Curry is spicy ◯

Telling Sentence	Asking Sentence

110 Complete English Success (Grade 2)

B. Put the words in order to write telling sentences.

Remember to begin each sentence with a capital letter and end it with a period.

1. on   is   the   nine   news   at   o'clock

   _____

2. the   it   winter   in   snows

   _____

3. made   glass   this   of   is   vase

   _____

4. are   the   sitting   they   at   table

   _____

C. Draw lines to match the two parts to form asking sentences.

1. When   •   • has left the scarf here?

2. Why   •   • is your birthday?

3. What   •   • you solve the puzzle?

4. Did   •   • can't penguins fly?

5. Who   •   • is that building?

6. How tall •   • is under the chair?

Complete English Success (Grade 2)

Section 2   Unit 11

An **exclamatory sentence** shows a strong emotion like fear, anger, or excitement. It ends with an exclamation mark (!).

An **imperative sentence** tells someone to do something. It ends with a period (.) or an exclamation mark (!).

Examples

Exclamatory Sentence

The cookies are so yummy!

Imperative Sentence

Please give me some more.

D. Check the circles to show whether the sentences are exclamatory or imperative.

	Exclamatory Sentence	Imperative Sentence
1. How lovely this flower is!	○	○
2. Pass me the book, please.	○	○
3. Never ever give up!	○	○
4. Oh no, I forgot my key!	○	○
5. Tell me the truth.	○	○
6. You look great!	○	○
7. Watch out!	○	○
8. Write your name here.	○	○
9. What a gorgeous view!	○	○
10. The fireworks are awesome!	○	○

E. Write what the children are saying.

A	**Imperative Sentence**

B	**Exclamatory Sentence**

C	**Telling Sentence**

D	**Asking Sentence**

Words That I Have Learned

Section 2 | Grammar

UNIT 12 Punctuation and Capitalization

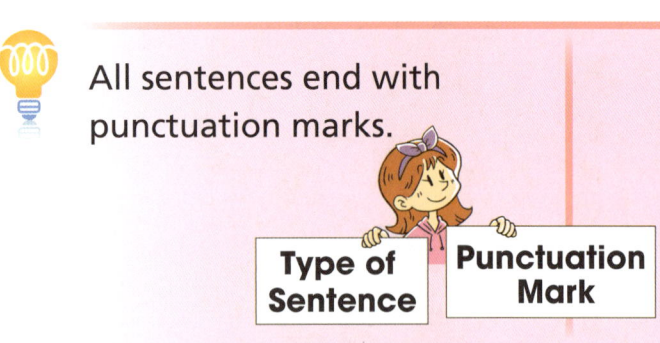

All sentences end with punctuation marks.

Examples
- Telling Sentence (.)
- Asking Sentence (?)
- Exclamatory Sentence (!)
- Imperative Sentence (. or !)

A. Circle the correct punctuation mark for each sentence.

1. What a wonderful show   . / !

2. Nobody is allowed to go there   . / ?

3. Are you excited to go shopping   ! / ?

4. Emily screamed with delight   . / ?

5. Drive slowly around schools   . / ?

6. Could you pass me the salt   ? / !

7. Pugs have big eyes   . / ?

8. How lovely   ? / !

9. Help   ? / !

B. Put the correct punctuation marks in the boxes.

1. Keep going ☐

2. Am I going to beat him ☐

3. I won't give up ☐

4. We ran the race last Friday ☐

5. How many of you joined the race ☐

6. What an exciting race ☐

7. Who won at last ☐

8. How lucky he is ☐

9. Never run right after lunch ☐

C. Check if the sentences end with the correct punctuation marks. If not, put the correct punctuation marks on the lines.

1. How amazing this is? ____

2. Run faster! ____

3. Are you good at painting! ____

4. Ouch, I'm hurt. ____

5. The clinic is on the second floor. ____

6. What good timing? ____

Section 2   Unit 12

 All sentences begin with **capital letters**. All proper nouns begin with capital letters, too. Names of people, pets, places, days, months, holidays, and titles of books, songs, and movies are all proper nouns.

Example

Jamie and I watched "The Puppet's Wish" at the Shining Star Theater.

D. Color the books that have titles with proper capitalization.

- beauty and the beast
- The Prince and the Pauper
- The Emperor's New Clothes
- Goldilocks and the Three Bears
- anne of green gables
- Jack and the Beanstalk

E. **Rewrite the sentences with proper capitalization and correct punctuation.**

1. last year's halloween was a friday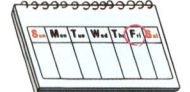

   _____

2. was mrs. jevon at home on new year's day

   _____

3. jennifer, ray, and i loved our picnic lunch

   _____

4. the concert was held in chicago last august

   _____

5. "we are the world" is such a great song

   _____

Words That I Have Learned

_____
_____
_____

Section 2 Grammar

UNIT 13 Forming Negative Sentences

The word "**not**" can be added to a sentence to form the negative.

Use "am/is/are not" to tell about something in the present.

Use "am/is/are not" and the "ing" form of a verb to tell about what is not going on.

Examples

- The boots <u>are not</u> new.

- It <u>is not raining</u>.

Negative Sentences

A. Read the sentences. Check the circles if they are negative sentences. Put a cross if they are not.

1. It is not very cold.

2. Alaia is playing the piano beautifully.

3. We are not invited to the party.

4. The boys are not cleaning their room.

5. I am not thirsty.

6.

I am so happy today!

118   Complete English Success (Grade 2)

Use "was/were not" to tell about a past state.

Use "was/were not" and the "ing" form of a verb to tell about what was not going on at a past time.

Examples

- He <u>was not</u> on our team last year.
- They <u>were not playing</u> outside when it rained.

B. Use ∧ to add "not" in the correct places to make the sentences negative.

1. Dad was using the computer earlier.

2. Zoey and Dennis were at the party last night.

3. They were singing when the bell rang.

4. Jacky was waiting for the bus at two o'clock yesterday.

5. We were looking when the clown came out.

6. Rachel and Percy were classmates last year.

7. The cherry pie we had this morning was very delicious.

8. Rhonda was at home when Jane called.

9. Sophia noticed that the machines were functioning well.

Section 2   Unit 13

To form a negative sentence with a singular subject except "I" and "you," add "does not" before the base form of a verb to talk about the present.

For a plural subject, "I," and "you," add "do not" before the base form.

Examples

- She <u>does not live</u> near her school.
- Penguins <u>do not fly</u>.

C.   Fill in the blanks to form negative sentences with the correct verbs.

> sleep   grow   stop   go
> like   want   know

1. The bus _____ here.

2. Jamie _____ fishing with his dad.

3. We _____ vegetables in our backyard.

4. Our pet dog _____ in my bedroom.

5. Check the map if you _____ where the arena is.

6. Mr. and Mrs. Moore _____ to live in the crowded city.

7. I _____ playing baseball.

To form a negative sentence to talk about the past, add "did not" before the base form of a verb with any subject.

Examples

- Jill <u>did not sing</u> at the party.
- They <u>did not watch</u> yesterday's game.

D. Rewrite the sentences as negative by changing the underlined verbs.

1.  Mom <u>went</u> to work last Saturday.

   _____

2. I <u>studied</u> in this school last year.

   _____

3.  Macy and Samuel <u>played</u> in the pool yesterday.

   _____

4. Jason <u>played</u> video games last night.

   _____

Words That I Have Learned

Section 2 | Grammar

Contractions

 A **contraction** is a short way of writing two words. One or more letters are replaced with an apostrophe (') in a contraction.

Examples
- you are → you're
- it is → it's

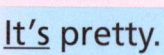 pretty.

A. Color the correct contractions of the words.

1. he is — he's | he'is
2. they are — they're | they'e
3. what is — wha's | what's
4. I have — I've | I'ave
5. there is — ther'is | there's
6. how is — how'is | how's
7. do not — do't | don't
8. they will — they'ill | they'll
9. you have — you've | you'e
10. does not — doesn't | does't
11. did not — didn't | did't
12. should not

    You should'nt | shouldn't eat so much candy.

B. **Check the circles if the contractions are spelled correctly. If not, cross out the words and write the correct spellings above them.**

1. I was'nt sure how I broke the toy. ○

2. Where'is the box office? ○

3. Isn'ot this your lunch bag? ○

4. What's in the basket? ○

5. Katie cann't finish the whole pizza. ○

6. Cecil didn't watch TV yesterday. ○

7. How'is everyone doing? ○

8. We're waiting for you now. ○

9. There are'nt any cookies left. ○

10. I'am happy to have you as my friend. ○

C. Circle the contractions. Then fill in the blanks with the correct contractions.

Contractions

couldn't	here's	Lily's	she's	we'd
weren't	James's	hasn't	to-do
cat's	a.m.	they'll	Dr.	why's

1. _____ very excited because she _____ seen such a big teddy bear before.

2. _____ a hint to help you crack the code.

3. The children _____ sleeping when their parents got home.

4. _____ better do some research before we build the model.

5. _____ finish the preparation by next Monday.

6. Jerry _____ see anything because there was no light in the room.

7. _____ it so very noisy outside?

D. Rewrite the sentences using contractions.

1. It is chasing a rat.

   _____

2. We will have fun at the pool.

   _____

3. That is the book I told you about.

   _____

4. Let us take a rest under the tree.

   _____

5. The children must not swim in the lake when no adults are around.

   _____

   _____

Words That I Have Learned

Contractions

_____

_____

_____

Review 2 — Grammar

A. **Circle the answers.**

1. "____" is a common noun.
   - City
   - Seattle
   - Boston

2. The plural of "box" is "____."
   - boxs
   - boxies
   - boxes

3. Which is correct?
   - The girls are eating honey.
   - The girls are eating honeys.
   - She is eating honeys.

4. Which phrase uses the correct article?
   - a sun
   - an sun
   - the sun

5. Which pronoun is correct?

   ____ want popcorn.

   - We
   - Them
   - Us

6. Which sentence is in the present tense?
   - The boy played.
   - The boy is playing.
   - The boy was playing.

7. Which adjective describes the picture?
   - round
   - square
   - tall

8. The tree is ____ the fence.
   - behind
   - beside
   - in

9. Which preposition is correct?

> Independence Day is _____ July.

on

in

at

10. Which one uses the correct joining word?

Are you staying or leaving today?

Are you staying and leaving today?

Are you staying but leaving today?

11. Which sentence has the predicate underlined?

<u>Ada</u> loves animals.

Ada <u>loves animals</u>.

Ada <u>loves</u> animals.

12. Which one below is an exclamatory sentence?

Do your homework!

We rock!

It is raining.

13. Which punctuation mark can an imperative sentence have?

. or !

! or ?

. or ?

14. The negative sentence for the sentence below is "_____"

> I like singing.

I doesn't like singing.

I do like singing.

I do not like singing.

Review 2 Grammar

Nouns and Pronouns

B. Write the underlined words in the correct boxes.

Long ago, there was a <u>kingdom</u> called <u>Colorland</u>. The <u>king</u>, <u>King Edwin</u>, and his people made sure it was a happy and colorful place. Their only problem was a naughty little <u>elf</u> named <u>Coby</u>.

One day, Coby took away all the colors! The people woke up to find that everything was black and white. Everyone tried in vain to look for Coby.

Common Noun

_____
_____
_____

Proper Noun

_____
_____
_____

C. Underline the subject pronouns and circle the object pronouns.

Then someone said, "Look what we have found! It is a note left for us by Coby."

To get all the colors back, Princess Lilian and Prince Ned have to search for one thing in each color. When they have found it, he or she needs to touch it and say its color! Then that color will return to the kingdom. I will be hiding somewhere nearby to make sure they follow the rules.

Coby

Tenses, Prepositions, and Joining Words

D. Circle the correct present tense and past tense verbs.

King Edwin carefully **studyied** / **studied** Coby's note. Then he said, "My children **are** / **am** very brave. I **am allow** / **am allowing** them to begin the search today!"

The king asked Wilkin to accompany the children. Wilkin had an idea, "We **are going** / **is going** to look all over the woods just outside Colorland before we **go** / **went** any farther."

E. Fill in the blanks with the correct prepositions and joining words.

1. The children came to a grassland _____ Colorland and the woods. Lilian touched the grass _____ said, "Green!" They got back the first color.

2. They searched the woods. Tired, they rested _____ a tree. Ned touched the tree trunk _____ the color brown returned.

3. Then a blue jay sat _____ Ned's shoulder. He touched it and got back the color blue.

Review 2 Grammar

The Sentence, Subjects, and Objects

F. Look at the picture. Then complete the sentences with the correct subjects or predicates.

1. _____ found the color orange!

2. _____ said "Pink!" as he ate a peach.

3. Wilkin _____ .

4. The children _____ .

G. Circle the subjects and underline the objects of the verbs.

The children gathered some fruits. They ate the oranges, peaches, and grapes. Lilian said, "I love fruits! But I am worried. How are we going to find yellow?"

"Look!" said Ned. They saw some roses. "Maybe they are yellow."

"But roses can be pink, red, or white, too," said Wilkin.

"That reminds me! We have to find red as well!" Lilian said in a panic.

Types of Sentences, Punctuation, and Capitalization

H. Identify the types of sentences. Write the letters.

A. What can we use to find red?

B. A ripe strawberry is always red.

C. I found a strawberry!

D. Touch it!

Sentences

○ Telling

○ Asking

○ Exclamatory

○ Imperative

I. Cross out the letters with the wrong capitalization and write the correct ones above them. Then put the appropriate punctuation in the circles.

after they had found the color red, the children retrieved the color yellow with a sunflower and returned to colorland ○

"let's celebrate ○ " cheered the people ○

"how have you been ○ " asked king edwin ○

"we are good ○ we had fun ○ " replied ned ○

"look ○ " said lilian as they saw coby disappear into thin air ○ he had left behind a book titled *magic spells* ○

Section 3
Vocabulary

 Scan this QR code or go to Download Center at **www.popularbookusa.com** to watch our fun videos on vocabulary!

 Antonyms

 Homophones

 Compound Words

Section 3   Vocabulary

UNIT 1

Sense Words

hear   hearing   see   sense   smell
sight   taste   touch

The Five Senses

Human beings have five senses: touch, smell, sight, hearing, and taste. We <u>touch</u> with our <u>hands</u>. That is how we know whether something is hot or cold, or hard or soft. We <u>smell</u> with our <u>nose</u>. We can tell whether something smells pleasant, like flowers, or unpleasant, like garbage. We <u>see</u> with our <u>eyes</u>, <u>hear</u> with our <u>ears</u>, and <u>taste</u> with our <u>tongue</u>.

A. Fill in the blanks with the underlined words.

1. I _____ with my 👀 _____.

2. I _____ with my 👃 _____.

3. I _____ with my 👂 _____.

4. I _____ with my ✋ _____.

5. I _____ with my 👅 _____.

B. Write the five senses. Then draw lines to match.

| The Five Senses | You can use more than one sense for some situations. |

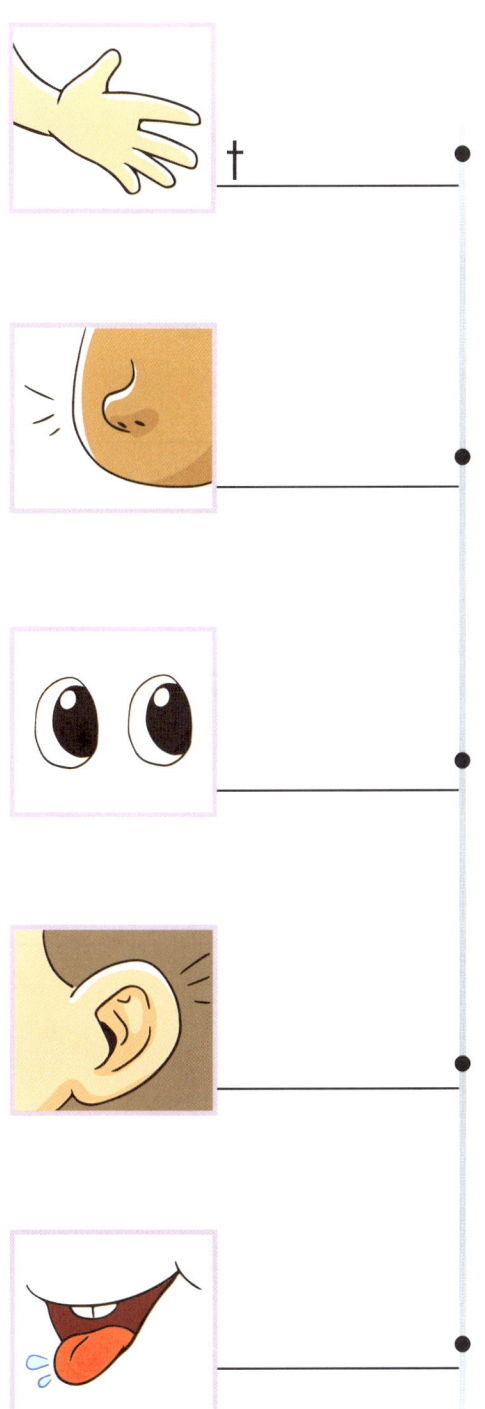

C. Write the correct words under the pictures.

Adjectives for the Sense of Touch

hot   cold   sticky   sharp   fluffy
hard   soft   smooth   rough

1.
h _____

2.
s _____

3.
f _____

4.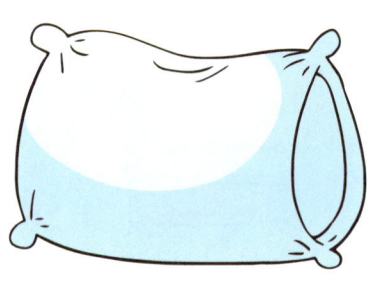
s _____

5.
c _____

6.
h _____

7.
r _____

8.
s _____

9.
s _____

D. Write the correct adjective for each food item. Then draw one more example.

Adjectives for the Sense of Taste

sweet **sour** **bitter** **salty** **spicy**

1. ______

2. ______

3. ______

4. ______

5. ______

Words That I Have Learned

Sense Words

______

______

______

Section 3 Vocabulary

UNIT 2 Season Words

| spring | summer | fall | winter |
| cold | cool | hot | warmer |

seasons

Different Seasons

There are four seasons in a year: spring, summer, fall, and winter.

Spring is the season when it gets warmer and rains more. Trees begin to bud in spring.

Summer is the season when the temperature gets high and it is hot. Leaves on trees are green in summer.

Fall is the season when leaves change color. Some leaves change from green to orange, yellow, red, and brown. The temperature drops and it is cool in fall.

Winter is the season when there is a lot of snow in most parts of North America. It is very cold and there are no more leaves on most trees in winter.

A. Name the seasons.

1. _____   2. _____   3. _____   4. _____

B. Fill in the blanks with the correct season words.

Season Words

| cold | hot | cool | warmer |
| breezy | snowy | sunny | rainy |

1. **Spring**
The temperature gets higher and it is _____ outside. It is a wet and _____ season.

2. **Winter**
The temperature drops a lot and it is very _____. It is _____ and everything is covered in white.

3. **Fall**
The temperature gets lower and it is _____ outside. It is a _____ season for flying kites.

4. **Summer**
The temperature gets very high and it is _____. It is a _____ season for playing at the beach.

C. **Draw lines to match the words with the same or similar meanings. Then find all the words in the word search.**

More Season Words

autumn •	• breezy
chilly •	• warm
windy •	• sunny
cozy •	• fall
scorching •	• cold
cloudless •	• hot

D. **Name your favorite season and draw a picture of it. Then fill in the blank and write two more sentences about it using season words.**

_____
my favorite season

My favorite season is _____ .

_____

_____

Words That I Have Learned

Season Words

_____

_____

_____

Complete English Success (Grade 2)

Section 3 Vocabulary

UNIT 3 Camping Words

backpack   barbecue   binoculars   blanket
camping   campsite   first aid kit   flashlight
rope   sleeping bag   s'more   tent

campfire

Family Camping

My family loves camping. Every summer, my sister and I pack our own backpacks for the camping trip. Dad makes sure to bring the tent, flashlights, binoculars, and a first aid kit. Mom packs our sleeping bags, blankets, ropes, and food for a barbecue.

When we arrive at the campsite, we all help set up the tent. Then we may swim, hike, or look at the wildlife with our binoculars. We then collect dry wood for the campfire.

At night, we have fun barbecuing, eating s'mores, and telling jokes by the fire.

A. Name the camping items.

Ⓐ _____

Ⓑ _____

Ⓒ _____

B. Draw lines to match the camping words with the pictures.

Camping Words

backpack •

barbecue •

binoculars •

blanket •

first aid kit •

s'more •

tent •

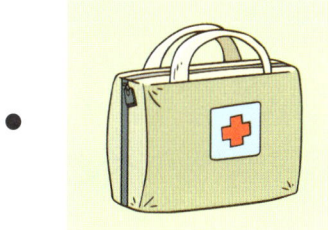

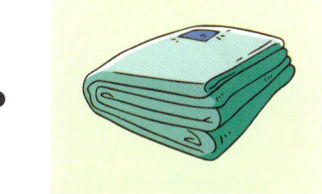

Section 3　Unit 3

C. Circle the correct spellings of the camping items.

More Camping Words

1.

marshmallo
marshmallow
marshmellow

2.

charcoal
chacoal
charcole

3.

compas
comppas
compass

4.

matchs
matches
mattchs

5.

boots
booots
bootes

6.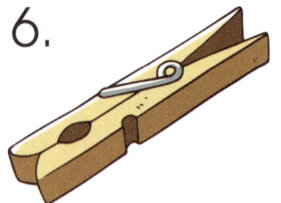

clothspin
clothpin
clothespin

7.

flaske
flask
fllask

8.

aex
ax
axx

9.

sunscreene
sunscrin
sunscreen

10.

lanten
lantern
lenten

D. Fill in the blanks with the correct words.

Camping Activities

wildlife watching   canoeing
stargazing   hiking

1. Many campsites are far away from city lights so they are perfect places for _____ .

2. _____ lets us learn about animals and plants in nature.

3. It is important to wear a pair of comfortable boots when _____ .

4. _____ was a way of traveling across water in the past, but today it has become a common camping activity.

Words That I Have Learned

Camping Words

_____

_____

_____

Section 3 Vocabulary
UNIT 4 Community Words

apartment building   bakery
bungalow   hospital   library
police station   school   supermarket
swimming pool   townhouse

my community

My Community

There are many different places in my community. My family and I live in a townhouse, but there are other types of homes, such as bungalows and apartment buildings.

There are schools and libraries where we learn about the world. A police station and a hospital provide us with emergency services. There are supermarkets, bakeries, and flower shops where we buy things to meet our daily needs. There are also eating places where we can enjoy dishes from around the world.

My favorite fun places to go with my family and friends are the park and the swimming pool.

A. Name the three types of living places.

1. _____   2. _____   3. _____

Complete English Success (Grade 2)

B. **Identify the community places. Name them or write the letters.**

A _____

B _____

C _____

D _____

E _____

F _____

G _____

H _____

I _____

J _____

K _____

more community places

○ post office

○ flower shop

○ gas station

○ dental clinic

○ restaurant

○ theater

Section 3 Unit 4

C. Draw lines to match the community workers with the places.

D. Fill in the blanks with the correct community words.

Community Place	Community Worker
convenience store	mail carrier
library theater	chef doctor

1. The _____ of this restaurant makes award-winning desserts.

2. You have to see the _____ when you feel sick.

3. There is a _____ near the cottage so we can buy some of the things we need there.

4. Maggie and her friends went to the _____ and saw an interesting movie last night.

5. Mom is waiting eagerly for the _____ to come and deliver a parcel from Aunt Daisy.

6. Oh no, I forgot to return these books to the _____ !

Words That I Have Learned

Community Words

_____

_____

_____

Section 3 Vocabulary

UNIT 5

Polygon Words

> heptagon   hexagon   octagon
> pentagon   quadrilateral   shape
> triangle   two-dimensional

Polygons

A polygon is a closed, two-dimensional shape with three or more straight sides. Circles and other shapes with curves are not polygons.

Polygons are named according to the number of sides they have. A polygon with three sides is called a triangle, one with four sides is called a quadrilateral, and one with five sides is called a pentagon. A six-sided polygon is a hexagon, a seven-sided one is a heptagon, and an eight-sided one is an octagon.

You can find polygons in many things around you. For example, a kite is a quadrilateral and a stop sign is an octagon.

A. Name the shapes. Then color the polygons.

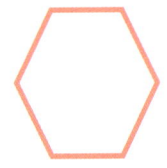      

1. _____   2. _____   3. _____

B. **Check the correct letters to name the polygons.**

1.

   A quadrilateral

   B hexagon

   C heptagon

2.

   A hexagon

   B triangle

   C quadrilateral

3.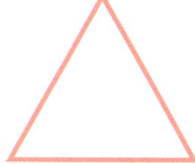

   A heptagon

   B octagon

   C triangle

4.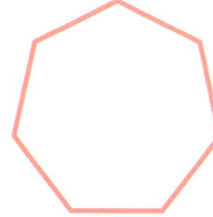

   A heptagon

   B hexagon

   C octagon

5.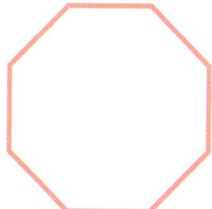

   A pentagon

   B hexagon

   C octagon

6.

   A triangle

   B pentagon

   C hexagon

   A pentagon

   B hexagon

   C octagon

C. Trace the polygons. Then write the number of sides and name the polygons.

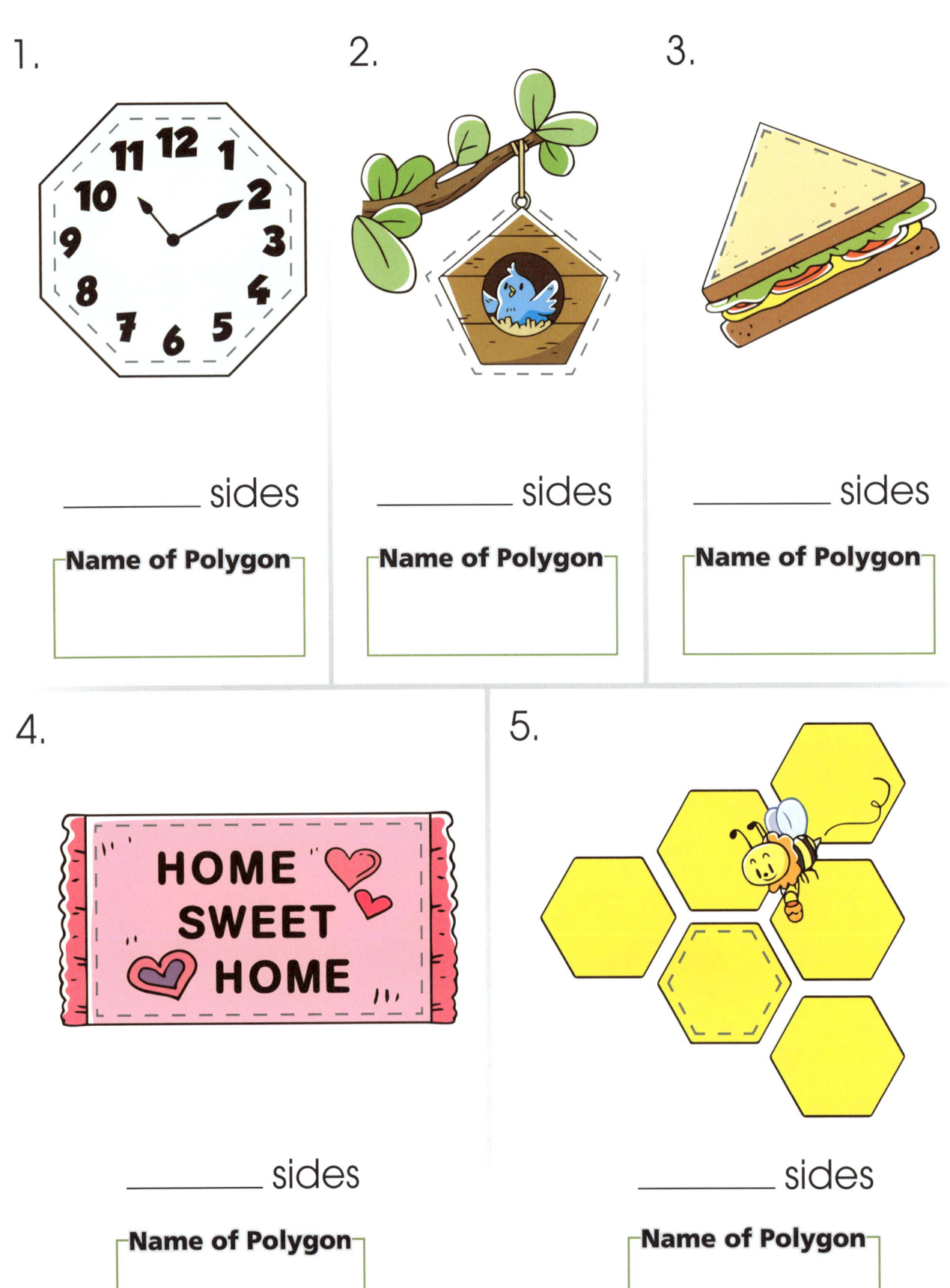

D. Look at each four-sided polygon. Draw a bigger one on the side and then name the polygon.

Quadrilaterals

square   rectangle   trapezoid   rhombus   parallelogram

Name

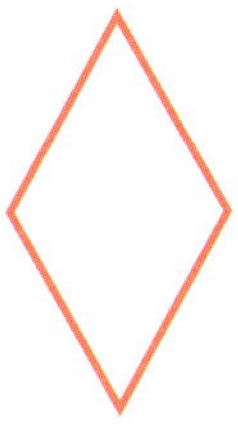

Name

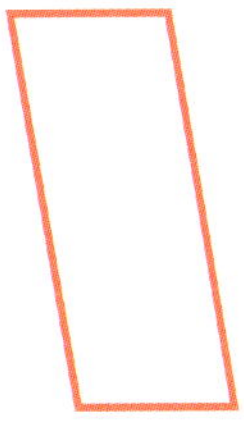

Name

Name

Name

Words That I Have Learned

Polygon Words

_____

_____

_____

Section 3 Vocabulary

UNIT 6 Computer Words

CPU   keyboard   modem
monitor   mouse   printer   screen

computer

The Computer

Computers are used everywhere – at home, at school, at the doctor's, at the dentist's, and in department stores. It is important to know the main parts of the computer. "CPU" is short for "Central Processing Unit," which is like the brain of the computer. The monitor is the screen that displays words and pictures. When you type on a keyboard, your words appear on the monitor. A mouse allows you to control a pointer on the screen to get your task done. If you want a paper copy, you can use a printer to print the words or pictures. If you add a modem to your computer, you can have access to the Internet.

A. Unscramble the words to name the parts of a computer.

1. imonrto _____

2. rcnese _____

3. domme _____

Complete English Success (Grade 2)

B. Name the parts of the computer.

Computer Words

| CPU | monitor | keyboard | mouse |
| printer | speakers | headphones | webcam |

I can listen to music with my _____.

Section 3   Unit 6

C. Match the computer icons with their functions. Write the letters.

Functions

A play/pause

B stop

C power on/off

D volume control

E brightness control

F battery level

G headphone jack

H music

I USB port

J settings

K mute

L tools

D. Fill in the blanks to show the uses of a computer.

Uses of a Computer

music   communicate   buy   photos   information

1. We can listen to _____ on the computer.

2. We can search for all kinds of _____ on various websites.

3. We can use the computer to _____ or sell things.

4. We can _____ with other people through email and social networks.

5. We can share _____ with our family and friends.

Words That I Have Learned

Computer Words

_____

_____

_____

Section 3 Vocabulary

Water Words

brook   creek   lake   ocean
river   sea   stream

Bodies of Water

There are different types of water bodies. The largest are oceans, which are large open areas of salt water. Many people refer to oceans as seas, but seas are in fact smaller than oceans and are connected to oceans. They are typically partially enclosed by land. Lakes are large bodies of water surrounded by land. Most lakes are freshwater. Ponds are also surrounded by land, but they are smaller than lakes.

There are flowing bodies of water, like rivers. Rivers flow into other rivers, lakes, or seas. Streams, creeks, and brooks are also flowing bodies of water, but they are narrower and shallower than rivers.

A. Unscramble the letters to name the water bodies.

1. _____ 2. _____
   eas   dopn

3. _____ 4. _____ 5. _____
   korbo   tearms   keal

6. _____ 7. _____ 8. _____
   rceke   virre   coane

B. Identify the oceans. Write the letters. Then fill in the blanks.

The Five Oceans of the World

○ Atlantic Ocean

○ Arctic Ocean

○ Indian Ocean

○ Pacific Ocean

○ Southern Ocean

1. The _____ is the largest and deepest of the world's oceans.

2. The smallest ocean is the _____ , which is around the North Pole.

3. The _____ lies south of Asia, with Africa and Australia on its sides.

4. The _____ is also known as the Antarctic Ocean. It surrounds Antarctica and is the southernmost ocean of the world.

5. The _____ lies east of North and South America.

Section 3   Unit 7

C. Look at the pictures and name the bodies of water.

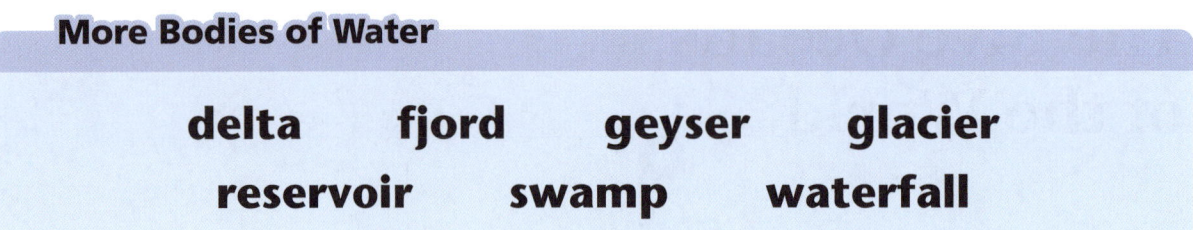

More Bodies of Water
delta   fjord   geyser   glacier
reservoir   swamp   waterfall

1. _____

2. _____

3. _____

4. _____

5. _____

6. _____

7. _____

D. Identify the shadows. Circle the correct names of the animals. Then draw lines to match if they are aquatic animals.

 whale / shark •

 octopus / jellyfish •

 cat / rabbit •   • **Aquatic Animals**

 crab / turtle •

 owl / squirrel •

 seal / crocodile •

Words That I Have Learned

Water Words

_____

_____

_____

Section 3 Vocabulary

UNIT 8 Synonyms

Synonyms are words with similar meanings.

beautiful – pretty   big – large
chose – picked   delicious – tasty – yummy
Mom – mother   sad – unhappy

glad – happy

Tasty Cupcakes

Dory was unhappy. She had lost her favorite dress. It was a beautiful red dress with a big, pretty bow. Her mother wanted to make her happy so she baked a batch of delicious cupcakes for Dory. Dory picked a large cupcake and then she chose one more. As soon as she tasted them, she said, "Thank you, Mom! They are so yummy!" Her mother was glad that Dory liked the cupcakes and that she was no longer sad.

A. Write the synonym(s) of each word.

tasty

sad

pretty

big

happy

Mom

picked

B. Write synonyms to describe the pictures.

> hungry　　frightened　　shiny
> 　　drowsy　　tiny

1.
scared
_____

2.
sparkly
_____

3.
small
_____

4.
sleepy
_____

5.
starving
_____

C. Circle the synonyms of the words in the boxes.

1. **friend**　　buddy　　neighbor　　pal

2. **jump**　　spin　　leap　　hop

3. **angry**　　furious　　patient　　mad

4. **clever**　　smart　　intelligent　　kind

5. **brave**　　cautious　　courageous　　bold

Complete English Success (Grade 2)

Section 3   Unit 8

D. **Fill in the blanks with the synonyms of the words under the lines.**

| fast | breezy | damp | hard | little |
| store | tired | huge | dirty | crying |

1. Cindy was _____ because she fell down.
   <u>weeping</u>

2. It was a _____ day in the city.
   <u>windy</u>

3. Mom was _____ after her trip.
   <u>exhausted</u>

4. The _____ child held on to the balloon.
   <u>small</u>

5. The weather was _____ and warm.
   <u>humid</u>

6. This _____ does not open on Sundays.
   <u>shop</u>

7. The kiwi fruit was _____ and green.
   <u>firm</u>

8. Becca ran _____ toward the finish line.
   <u>quickly</u>

9. The bike tires were _____ after they went
   <u>grimy</u>
   through the mud.

10. Mike found a _____
    <u>giant</u>
    zucchini in the garden.

E. **Rewrite the sentences using the correct synonyms for the underlined words.**

| pails | bunny | shut | weird | awesome |

1. Little Ryan loves the fluffy <u>rabbit</u>.

   _____

2. Please <u>close</u> the door behind you.

   _____

3. Did you hear that <u>strange</u> noise?

   _____

4. Hana's performance was <u>amazing</u>.

   _____

5. Let's fill the <u>buckets</u> with water.

   _____

Words That I Have Learned

Synonyms

_____

_____

_____

Section 3   Vocabulary

UNIT 9 Antonyms

Antonyms are words with opposite meanings.

cold – hot   day – night   dry – wet
less – more   long – short

thick   thin

The Cactus

The cactus plant grows in the desert where it is hot during the day and cold at night. There is more sunshine and less rainfall in the desert than many other places in the world. When it does rain for short periods of time, the shallow plant roots soak up rainwater from the wet ground. The stem of the cactus plant is thick with thin, prickly thorns on it. This means that the plant can store water for when the ground is dry for long periods of time.

A. Color each pair of antonyms with the same color.

(hot)   (thick)   (wet)   (thin)   (day)   (short)

(night)   (less)   (cold)   (long)   (dry)   (more)

B. For each group of words, cross out the one that is not an antonym of the word on the left.

above

1. dirty — clean — messy — tidy
2. give — take — provide — receive
3. scared — bold — brave — afraid
4. end — start — begin — open
5. short — large — tall — high
6. smooth — rough — rugged — plain

below

C. Match the antonyms. Write the letters.

A bent
B cry
C question
D empty
E strong

◯ answer
◯ straight
◯ full
◯ weak
◯ laugh

D. Write each word in the box with its antonym.

> go   fast   depart   difficult   glad   hard
> correct   happy   swift   right   speedy
> leave   proper   jolly   challenging

stay

sad

slow

wrong

easy

E. **Circle the antonyms in the sentences. Then write them on the lines.**

1. Betsy left home early so that she would not be late for the fun event.

2. The best time to fly a kite is on a calm day and the worst time is on a windy day.

3. Derek opened his eyes when the hot-air balloon went up, but he closed them when it came down.

Antonyms

1. _____ _____

2. _____ _____

3. _____ _____
   _____ _____
   _____ _____

Words That I Have Learned

Antonyms

_____

_____

_____

Section 3 | Vocabulary

UNIT 10
Homophones

Homophones are words that sound the same but have different spellings and meanings.

blew – blue   dear – deer
road – rode   sea – see
son – sun   tail – tale   too – two

Amar and His Son

Amar and his son had a lot of fun on Sunday. In the morning, they got up early to see the sun rise in the mountains. Then they each had two eggs for breakfast. They had sausages, too. In the afternoon, they rode their bikes along a trail away from the road. They were excited to come across a deer. Then they sat by the sea under the blue sky. The wind blew lightly as Amar told his son a tale about a tiger with a soft, fluffy tail. At night, Amar said to his son, "Good night, my dear, brave knight!" And he switched off the lights and went to sleep.

A. Write the homophones of the words.

1. road _____ 2. two _____

3. blue _____ 4. son _____

5. tail _____ 6. see _____

7. night _____ 8. dear _____

B. Draw lines to match the homophones.

- flower •
- one •
- mail •
- rain •
- plane •
- meat •
- pear •
- key •

• reign

• flour

• plain

• meet

• quay

• pair

• male

• won

Section 3 Unit 10

C. **Write the correct homophones of the words under the lines.**

1. The _____ lives in the woods.
   bare

2. We _____ the corn.
   eight

3. Mary walked _____ the car.
   buy

4. It takes 100 _____ to make a dollar.
   sense

5. The doctor checks my _____ .
   wait

6. She _____ the answer.
   new

7. Can you _____ the music?
   here

8. The girl took _____ nuts.
   sum

9. Judy picked the _____ .
   flour

10. Will she _____ the candy to me?
    cell

11. I got stung by a _____ !
    be

12. I will _____ my name on the card.
    right

D. **Rewrite the sentences by replacing the underlined words with the correct homophones.**

1. Kelly taught us how to tie a <u>not</u>.

   _____

   _____

2. I picked berries on my <u>weigh</u> to Grandma's house.

   _____

   _____

3. Ricky played basketball for an <u>our</u>.

   _____

   _____

4. The <u>hair</u> hopped away when we got closer.

   _____

   _____

Words That I Have Learned

Homophones

_____

_____

_____

Review 3 Vocabulary

A. **Circle the answers.**

1. We use our sense of ___ to see.
   hearing
   touch
   sight

2. In which season does the snow fall?
   summer
   fall
   winter

3. Which camping word is spelled correctly?
   compase
   compass
   compas

4. Which is not a community word?
   apartment
   building
   townhouse
   flask

5. Where does a baker work in a community?
   in a bakery
   in a library
   in a hospital

6. What polygon is this?
   hexagon
   octagon
   pentagon

7. What is the function of this computer icon?
   volume control
   power on/off
   brightness control

8. To which category does the word "information" belong?
   a community word
   a polygon word
   a computer word

9. Which is a frozen body of water?

    a glacier

    a swamp

    an ocean

10. What body of water is this?

    a fjord

    a delta

    a geyser

11. The synonym of "sleepy" is "___."

    relaxed

    drowsy

    active

12. Which is not a synonym of the word "friend"?

    neighbor

    pal

    buddy

13. The antonym of "scared" is "___."

    brave

    frightened

    afraid

14. The antonym of "stay" is "___."

    stayed

    left

    leave

15. The words "hour" and "___" are homophones.

    our

    flower

    hours

16. The words "weight" and "___" are homophones.

    wheat

    eight

    wait

Sense, Season, and Camping Words

B. Read the story. Then write the underlined words in the correct boxes.

We went camping in the middle of fall. It was a beautiful but chilly day. I could see the autumn colors and hear the birds chirping. My brother Dilan and I put on our boots and jackets and helped Mom set up the tent. Then we filled our backpacks with sweet and salty snacks and went canoeing. It got a bit windy so we headed back to our campsite. Then we made s'mores and barbecued by the campfire. I felt so happy and cozy sitting on a smooth rock. Before sleeping, we used our binoculars for stargazing as it was a cloudless night. It was the best camping trip!

Sense Word	Season Word	Camping Word

Community and Polygon Words

C. Read what the people say and draw lines to show where they should go.

1. I need to pick up a package that my aunt sent me from England.
2. I want to buy flowers for my mom.
3. I need someone to take care of my child while I am at work.
4. I have been feeling sick all week.

- hospital
- daycare
- post office
- flower shop

D. Look at the pictures and write the correct polygon words.

octagon   triangle   pentagon   rhombus   rectangle

1. 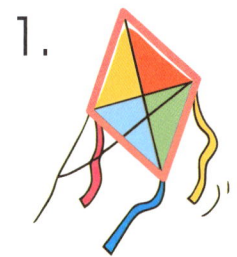 _____

2. 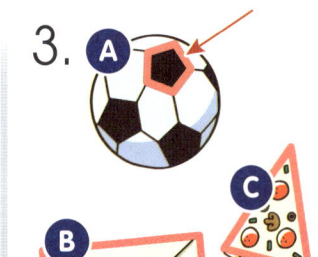 _____

3.
   A _____
   B _____
   C _____

Review 3   Vocabulary

Computer Words

E. Fill in the blanks to complete the sentences.

1. The _____ displays words and pictures.

2. The _____ is the "brain" of the computer.

3. You can use a _____ to type.

4. The _____ allows you to control the pointer on the screen.

Water Words

F. Label the picture with the correct water words.

waterfall   pond   delta   turtle   river

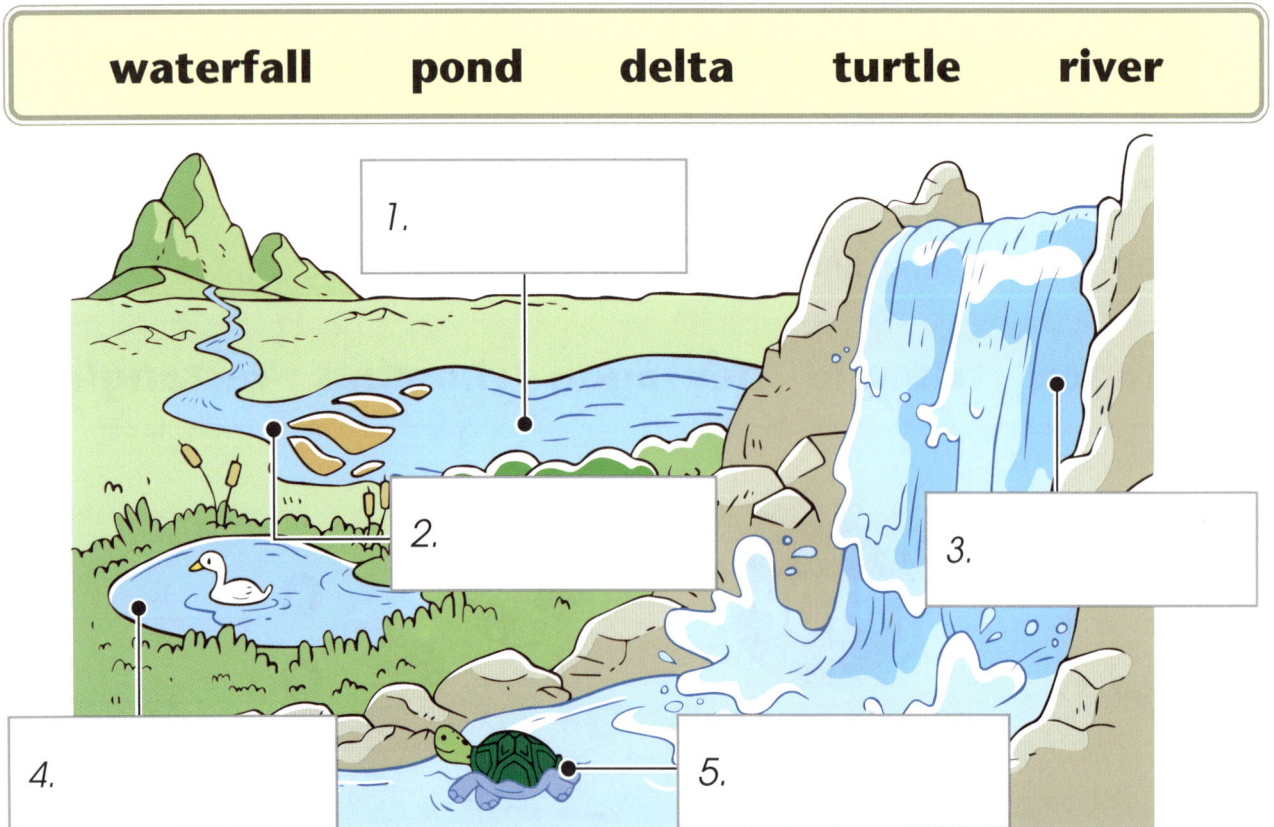

Synonyms and Antonyms

G. Complete the crossword puzzle with the synonyms or antonyms of the clue words.

Across

Synonyms
- A quickly
- B clever
- C scared
- D little
- E sad
- F hungry

Down

Antonyms
- 1 rough
- 2 easy
- 3 empty
- 4 day
- 5 slow
- 6 question

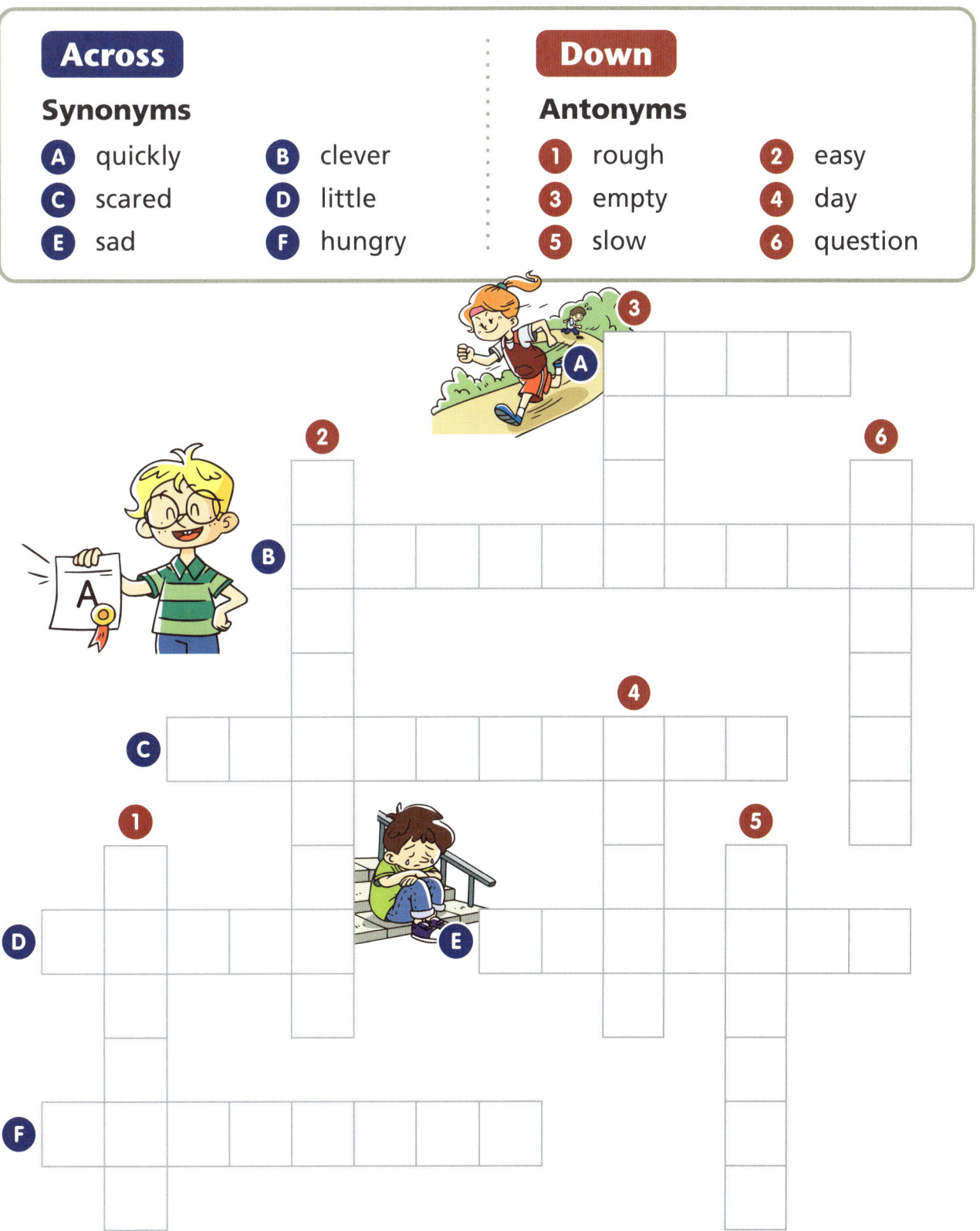

Section 4
Reading and Writing

Scan this QR code or go to Download Center at **www.popularbookusa.com** to watch our fun videos on reading and writing!

 Be a Detective

 Hilarious Name Puns

 Comics

Section 4 **Reading and Writing**

UNIT 1

A Balloon Ride

It was a sunny morning. Janet got out of bed early because she was going for a ride in a hot-air balloon. "I'm so excited!" she said. "Get ready quickly!" her mom told her. Then they left home for the big adventure.

The colorful balloon waited in the park. Janet jumped into the basket and said, "I'm ready to fly!" The man in the basket used a burner to make the air hot. The balloon began to lift off slowly and up they went into the sky. Janet felt like a bird flying over the tops of trees and houses!

A. Draw lines to match who said what.

Janet's mom

Janet

- "Get ready quickly!"

- "I'm ready to fly!"

- "I'm so excited!"

B. Circle the answers.

1. How does Janet feel?

   scared

   sad

   excited

2. What does Janet ride in?

3. Who is with Janet?

   her mom

   her dad

   her brother

4. What does the balloon fly over?

   clouds

   birds

   trees

C. Answer the questions.

1. What is the setting of the story?

    The setting of a story is the place and time of the events.

   _____

2. What is the big adventure?

   _____

3. Describe the hot-air balloon.

   _____

Section 4   Unit 1

D. Read the story on page 182 again. Then write the information and circle the correct picture and word.

1. Title: _____

2. Characters: _____
   _____

3. Place:

4. Time of the Day: **morning / afternoon / night**

E. Read the text and cross out the sentences that do not belong.

 Sentences in a text have to be related to make sense.

Hot-air Balloon

There is a burner in the hot-air balloon. The burner has to be lit. You can light candles with matches. It heats up the air in the balloon. The children played a ball game. The hot air makes the balloon rise into the sky.

F. **Read the sentences and cross out the ones that do not belong. Then write the sentences in order and use sequence words to link them.**

> You can use words such as "before," "after," and "then" to show the sequence of the events.

- **A** Janet got up early.
- **B** She had a nightmare.
- **C** _____ she got ready and went to the park.
- **D** _____ the man lit the burner, Janet jumped into the basket.
- **E** _____ the balloon lifted off, Janet felt like a bird flying.
- **F** Some birds have wings but cannot fly.

_____
_____
_____
_____

Words That I Have Learned

_____
_____
_____

UNIT 2 The Sun and the Ocean

"Grandpa, why does the rain fall?" asked Toby. His grandpa said, "I asked my grandma the same question. Here is what she told me. The rain falls because of something that happened a long time ago. The Sun and the Ocean were best friends. One day, the Ocean wanted to visit the Sun on the tall mountain. So he turned himself into clouds and rose to the mountain. The Ocean stayed with his friend there, but every time the Ocean misses his home, he turns into water again and falls down as rain to the earth below."

A. Check if the sentences are true. If not, put a cross.

1. Toby wants to know why the rain falls.
2. Toby's grandma tells him the story.
3. The Sun and the Mountain are best friends.
4. The Ocean turns into clouds.
5. The Ocean's home is on the mountain.

B. Circle the answers.

1. Who told Grandpa the story?

   Toby

   Toby's grandma

   Grandpa's grandma

2. The Sun and the Ocean are ___ .

   brothers

   cousins

   friends

3. Who visits the Sun?

   the Ocean

   the mountain

   the rain

4. Who are the main characters of the story?

C. Answer the questions.

1. Is "The Sun and the Ocean" a folktale?

    A folktale is a story passed on by people through speech.

   _____

2. Where does the rain fall?

   _____

3. When does the Ocean turn into rain?

   _____

D. Draw lines to match the sentences with the pictures. Then put the sentences in order. Write the letters in the circles.

A The clouds rain onto the earth below.

B The Ocean turns into clouds.

C The Sun and the Ocean are best friends.

D The clouds rise up to where the Sun is on the mountain.

In order:

E. **Write the sentences in order to continue the story "The Sun and the Ocean." Then draw a picture to go with it.**

- Then the Sun wants to visit the Ocean.
- The Ocean becomes himself again.
- The next morning, the Sun leaves his friend.
- The rain falls down to the earth.
- He rises high up in the sky again.
- He sets at dusk to meet his friend.

The rain _____

_____

_____

_____

_____

_____

_____

Words That I Have Learned

Section 4 Reading and Writing

UNIT 3 The Museum Trip

Dear Aunt Meg,

I hope you are doing well.

Yesterday, our class went on a trip to the American Museum of Natural History (AMNH) in New York City. We left school at nine o'clock in the morning and returned at three o'clock in the afternoon.

When we got to the museum, we visited the Hall of Ocean Life. There was a gigantic blue whale there. It was awesome! We also visited the dinosaurs and the Rose Center for Earth and Space.

Today, when we got back to school, we drew and wrote about what we saw in the museum. I have learned a lot from this trip. Let's go to the museum when you visit us in New York this summer.

Sincerely,
Todd

A. Write what Todd saw in the museum.

1.  2.  3.

_____   _____   _____

B. **Circle the answers.**

1. What is the AMNH?

   a school

   a library

   a museum

2. Who goes on the trip with Todd?

   his classmates

   his parents

   his aunt

3. Where will Todd take his aunt the next time she visits them in summer?

   to the AMNH

   to his school

   to New York City

4. What time does the trip end?

C. **Answer the questions.**

A letter begins with "Dear ___" to tell who receives it. The sender's name appears at the bottom of the letter.

1. Write the answers.

   Sender: _____

   Receiver: _____

2. What is the full name of the AMNH?

   _____

3. What does Todd do in school after the trip?

   _____

Section 4   Unit 3

D. Fill in the blanks to complete the letter about a trip. Then draw your face in the circle.

My Letter

Dear _____ ,
         receiver

I hope you are doing well. I am writing to tell you about my trip to _____ .
                                                                      name of place

I went there on _____ with
                  date and month

_____ . Some of the things we
people you went with

did there were _____

_____

_____ .

I cannot wait for you to visit me. Then we can go on a trip together!

Sincerely,

_____
    your name

E. Address the envelope and draw a stamp to go with it.

You need an envelope with a stamp and addresses to send a letter.

_____ ← sender's name

_____ ⎱ sender's
_____ ⎰ address

_____ ← receiver's name

_____ ⎱ receiver's
_____ ⎰ address

Words That I Have Learned

_____

_____

_____

Section 4 Reading and Writing

UNIT 4 Alphabet Rhyme

A is for ape.

B is for bike.

C is for cape

And D is for dike.

I is for inn.

J is for jam.

K is for kin

And L is for lamb.

E is for ear.

F is for five.

G is for gear

And H is for hive.

M is for more.

N is for net.

O is for oar

And P is for pet.

A. Write what the pictures are with words from the rhyme.

1.

2.

3.

_____   _____   _____

B. **Circle the answers.**

1. How many rhyming pairs are there?

    four

    six

    eight

2. There are ___ lines in the poem.

    12

    16

    26

3. Which word rhymes with "inn"?

    kin

    dike

    hive

4. Which one rhymes with "ear"?

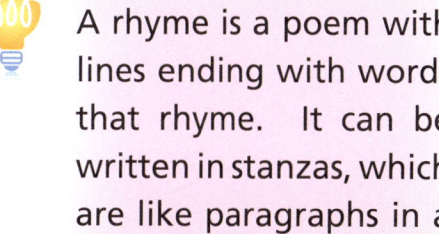
A rhyme is a poem with lines ending with words that rhyme. It can be written in stanzas, which are like paragraphs in a written text.

C. **Answer the questions.**

1. What type of text is this?

    _____

2. How many stanzas are there in this rhyme?

    _____

3. List the rhyming pairs.

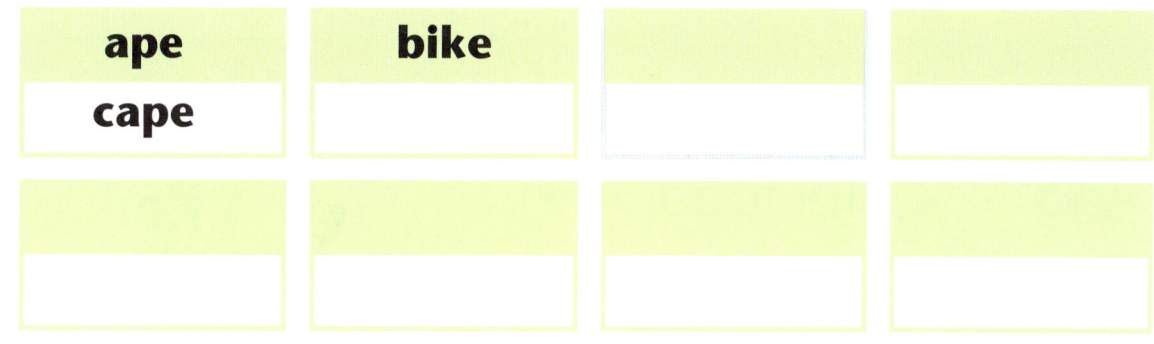

ape	bike		
cape			

Section 4   Unit 4

 Stanzas in a rhyme follow a rhyme scheme. A stanza has the ABAB scheme when:
- the first and the third lines rhyme, and
- the second and the fourth lines rhyme.

e.g. A is for <u>ape</u>. ← A
B is for bike. ← B
C is for <u>cape</u> ← A
And D is for dike. ← B

D. Complete the stanza following the ABAB scheme. Then draw pictures to go with it.

☐ is for quail.

R is for _____ .

S is for _____

And ☐ is for toad.

E. Complete the rhyme from A to H following the AABB scheme.

Alphabet Rhyme

A stanza with the AABB scheme:
- the first and the second lines rhyme
- the third and the fourth lines rhyme

A _____

B _____

C _____

And D _____

E _____

F _____

G _____

And H _____

Words That I Have Learned

_____

_____

_____

Section 4 Reading and Writing

UNIT 5 — Today Is My Birthday!

Hooray!

Today is my seventh birthday!

I will help my mother bake

A big pink strawberry cake!

All my friends will sing

And I will be like a king!

We will eat, play, and run

And have lots of birthday fun!

A. Read the poem. Then color the correct cake using the color mentioned in the poem and draw the correct number of candles.

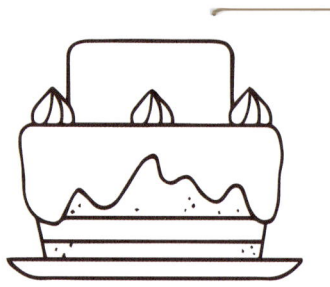

B. Circle the answers.

1. When is the writer's birthday?

   yesterday

   today

   tomorrow

2. How old is the writer?

   five years old

   six years old

   seven years old

3. Who will sing at the party?

   the writer

   the writer's mother

   the writer's friends

4. With whom will the writer bake a cake?

Mother   Father   Friend

C. Answer the questions.

1. Why is the writer happy?

   _____

2. What will the children do at the birthday party?

   _____

3. List the rhyming pairs in the poem.

   _____   _____

   _____   _____

D. Read the poem. Then color the boxes to show its characteristics.

My Birthday

This year my birthday

Falls on a Sunday!

I will be very glad

To spend time with my dad.

And Mom will be there

With us in the open air.

We will play in the sun

And have lots of fun!

Characteristics of the Poem

This poem has a title.

This poem has short sentences.

This poem has rhyming words.

This poem follows the ABAB scheme.

This poem follows the AABB scheme.

This poem describes items.

This poem describes feelings.

E. Look at the picture and write a short poem about it. Give your poem a title and make sure it follows a rhyme scheme.

Some Words You May Use

stars	clown	balloons
dots	happy	shiny

_____
Title of the Poem

_____
_____
_____
_____
_____
_____
_____

Words That I Have Learned

_____
_____
_____

Section 4　Reading and Writing

UNIT 6　The Butterfly's Life Cycle

All living things have a life cycle. They are born, they grow up, they lay eggs or have babies, and they die. Butterflies have an interesting life cycle.

The Butterfly's Life Cycle

Egg — A tiny egg is laid on a leaf.

Caterpillar — The egg hatches and becomes a caterpillar. The caterpillar eats a lot and becomes big.

Pupa — It forms a cover around itself and becomes a pupa.

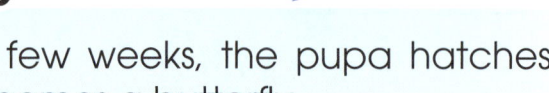

Butterfly — After a few weeks, the pupa hatches and becomes a butterfly.

A. Write 1 to 4 to put the events in order.

B. **Circle the answers.**

1. What does the egg hatch into?

   a caterpillar

   a pupa

   a butterfly

2. The caterpillar is covered when it becomes ____ .

   an egg

   a pupa

   a butterfly

3. The caterpillar eats a lot before becoming ____ .

   a pupa

   an egg

   a butterfly

4. What turns directly into a butterfly?

C. **Answer the questions.**

1. What is the title of the graphic text?

   _____

A graphic text uses diagrams/pictures and words to show information.

2. What is the text about?

   _____

3. How many pictures are there? What do they show?

   _____

D. Write a title for the diagram. Label and draw arrows to complete it. Then identify its characteristics and check the circles.

Title: _____

_____

_____

_____

_____

Characteristics of a Diagram

 A diagram is a type of graphic text.

○ legend   ○ arrows

○ compass   ○ text

○ title   ○ color

○ labels   ○ pictures

E. Read the sentences. Then draw and color a diagram to show the life cycle of the sunflower.

 A seed falls on the ground.

 A bud appears and the flower opens.

 Roots come out.

 The seed grows into a shoot and leaves appear.

 The flower dies and the seeds fall on the ground.

Title: _____

Words That I Have Learned

_____

_____

_____

Section 4 Reading and Writing

UNIT 7 Crispy Squares

Crispy Square Recipe

Ingredients

- 5 cups of rice crispies
- 1 packet of marshmallows
- $\frac{1}{2}$ cup of margarine

Directions

1. Melt the margarine in the saucepan; add the marshmallows and keep stirring until they melt.
2. Mix this mixture with the rice crispies in the large bowl.
3. Pat into the greased baking dish and cool it in the refrigerator.
4. Cut into squares.

Utensils

 large bowl

 saucepan

 spatula

 baking dish

 measuring cup

A. Read the recipe. Then write 1 to 4 to put the steps in order.

B. **Circle the answers.**

1. Which step below requires heat?

   Step 1

   Step 2

   Step 3

2. Which item is used for measuring?

   baking dish

   spatula

   measuring cup

3. A utensil is _____ .

   a clothing item

   a kitchen tool

   a furniture item

4. Which item is not an ingredient in the recipe?

C. **Answer the questions.**

 Instructions are informational texts that provide step-by-step directions to teach you how to do something.

1. Why is this recipe an informational text?

   _____

2. What ingredients are needed to make crispy squares?

   _____

3. What is the use of the spatula in this recipe?

   _____

D. Look at the diagram. Then complete the recipe.

How to Make a Smoothie

It is important to use all the ingredients and follow the directions.

1 peeled banana
2 ice cubes
1 cup of milk
4 strawberries

Put the ingredients into the blender.

Blend for one minute.

Pour the smoothie into a glass.

_____ Recipe

Ingredients

_____
_____
_____
_____

Utensils

_____
_____
_____

Directions

1 _____

2 _____

3 _____

E. Draw a picture of a simple food item. Then write the ingredients, utensils, and directions needed to make it.

_____ Recipe

Ingredients

Directions

Utensils

Words That I Have Learned

Section 4 **Reading and Writing**

UNIT 8

Jumbo the Gigantic Elephant

In the early 1880s, there was an enormous elephant named Jumbo. He was named by a zookeeper of the London Zoo after the Swahili word "jumbe," which means "chief." Almost 100,000 children wrote to Queen Victoria to stop him from being sold. However, Jumbo was sold to Barnum and Bailey Circus, an American traveling circus, and became a star of their show. He was so huge that he could carry up to 100 children on his back at one time!

A. Draw lines to match the words with their meanings.

Word	Meaning
1. jumbe	• very big
2. almost	• chief
3. enormous	• nearly
4. star	• famous performer

B. **Circle the answers.**

1. What was the queen's name?

   Elizabeth

   Alexandra

   Victoria

2. "Jumbe" is a word in the ___ language.

   Swahili

   circus

   English

3. Who was the star of the circus?

   Jamie

   Jumbo

   Jumbe

4. Barnum and Bailey was a ___ .

C. **Answer the questions.**

1. When was Jumbo kept at the London Zoo?

   _____

   _____

Informational texts contain facts such as dates, numbers, and names.

2. How many children could Jumbo carry?

   _____

3. Who gave Jumbo his name?

   _____

D. Read the informational text and fill in the facts.

Jumbo's Accident

On one of his trips with Barnum and Bailey Circus, Jumbo was struck by a train in an accident. This happened on September 15, 1885 in St. Thomas, Ontario, Canada. At that time, Jumbo was trying to save the life of a young elephant named Tom Thumb, who had wandered near the train tracks. A life-size statue of Jumbo was put up in St. Thomas in 1985.

Facts about Jumbo's Accident

Date of the Accident: _____

Place of the Accident: _____ _____
                          city   province

                         _____
                          country

Whom Jumbo Wanted to Save: _____

What Jumbo Was Struck by: _____

When Jumbo's Statue Was Erected: _____

Where Jumbo's Statue Was Erected: _____

E. **Complete the facts about yourself. Then draw or paste a picture of yourself in the box.**

Facts about Me

My name is _____ .

I was born on _____
 date

in _____ , _____ . My family and
 city country

I live in _____ . I am ____ years old.
 state age

I have _____ eyes and _____ hair.
 color color

I have ____ siblings.
 number

Words That I Have Learned

_____

_____

_____

Complete English Success (Grade 2)

Bat Facts

Bats are interesting animals. They are the only mammals that can fly. Like other mammals, they give birth to live young.

Habitat

Bats live in almost every country in the world. They live in places with mild temperatures – where it is not very hot or very cold.

Diet

Bats usually eat fruits or insects. Vampire bats eat the blood of dead birds and cattle.

Senses

Bats have good hearing. This helps them find food. They see best in the dark, which is when they hunt for food.

A. Check the correct sentences.

1. Bats are flying mammals.

2. Mammals can fly and give birth to live young.

3. A habitat is the home of an animal.

4. "Diet" means what someone eats.

5. Bats can see best in the morning light.

B. **Circle the answers.**

1. Mild temperatures are ____ temperatures.

   very hot

   very cold

   not very hot or cold

2. What helps a bat find food?

   its hearing

   its flying skills

   its sense of taste

3. When do bats hunt?

   in the morning

   in the afternoon

   at night

4. What do bats usually eat?

C. **Answer the questions.**

An informational text tells you the facts about someone or something. These facts are sometimes put under different subheadings.

1. Does the text contain facts or fiction?

   _____

2. What are the subheadings in the text?

   _____

3. How can you tell that bats are mammals?

   _____

D. Read the text and cross out the sentences that are not facts. Then rewrite the text as an informational text.

A Bat's Hearing

A bat flies at night without crashing. ~~This is because bats are magical animals.~~ It makes noise and listens for it to bounce back. This noise is called an echo. ~~An echo is created by an enchanted wand.~~ The echo tells a bat where an object is. Then the bat can avoid the object. ~~That is why no bats have crashed into the witch's castle.~~

A Bat's Hearing

_____
_____
_____
_____
_____
_____

E. Write an informational text about an animal. Then draw a picture to go with it.

_____ **Facts**

Habitat

_____

_____

_____

_____

_____

_____

_____

_____

Words That I Have Learned

_____

_____

_____

Section 4 Reading and Writing

UNIT 10 Big Red Rescuer

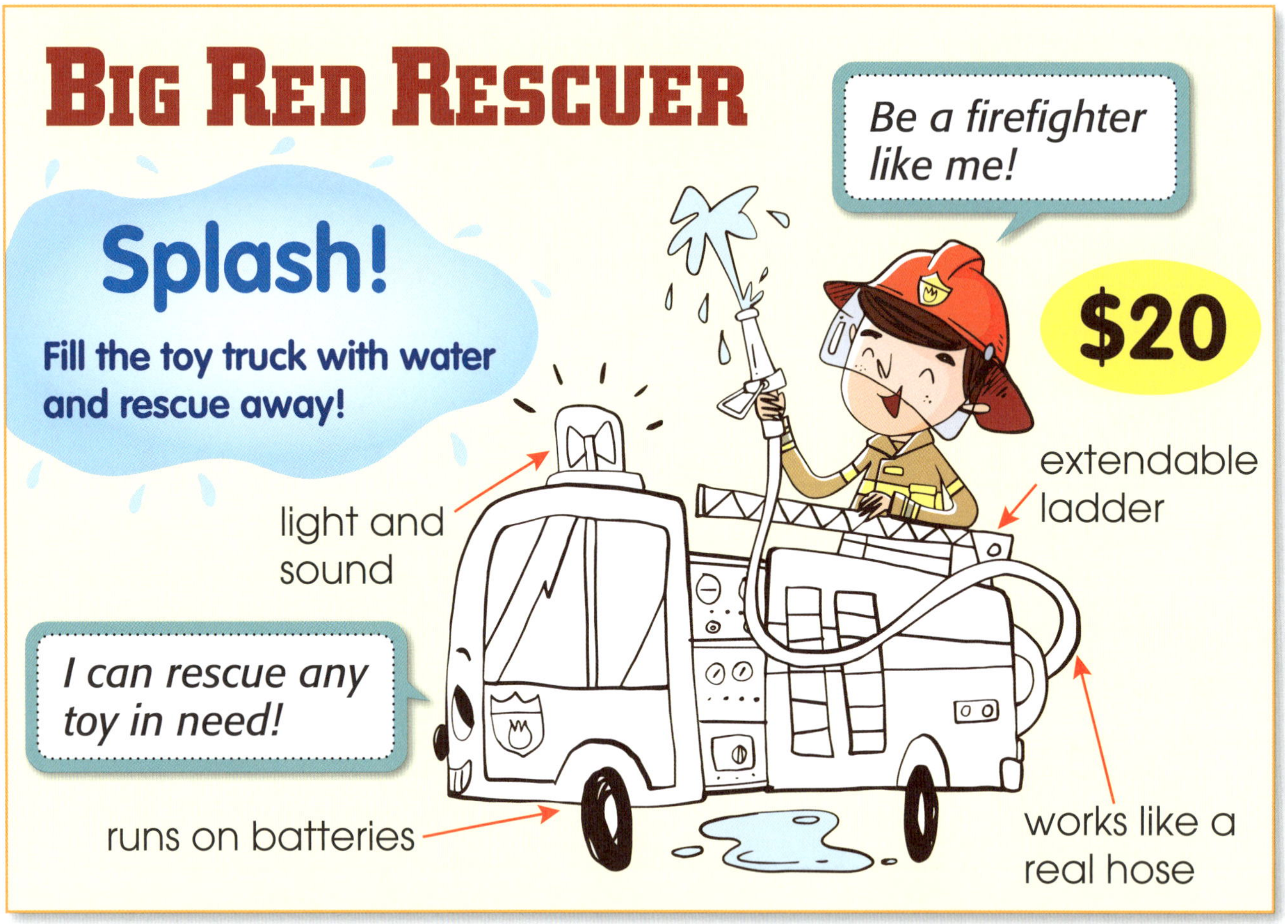

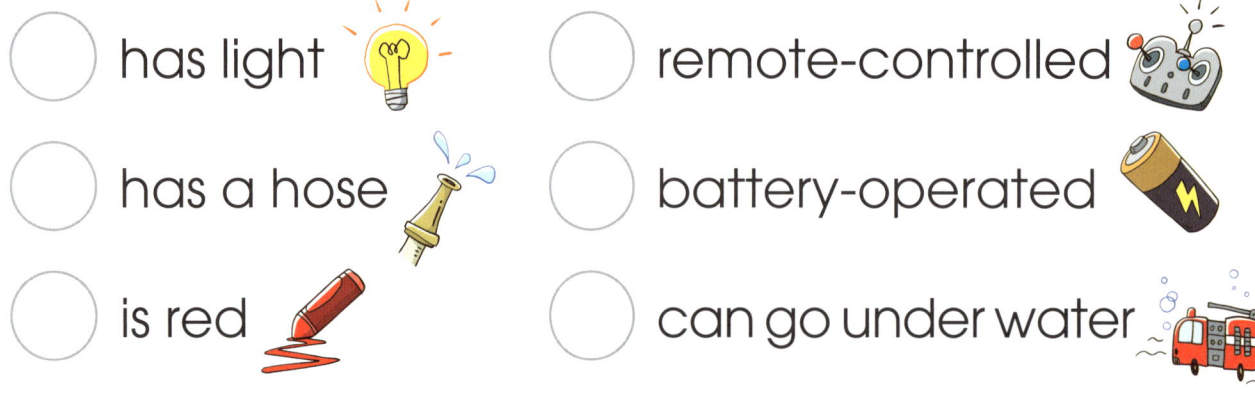

A. Check the features of the fire truck. Then color the truck.

- ○ has light
- ○ has a hose
- ○ is red
- ○ has sound
- ○ remote-controlled
- ○ battery-operated
- ○ can go under water
- ○ has an extendable ladder

B. **Circle the answers.**

1. "Splash" refers to the sound of ____ .

    the hose

    the truck

    water

2. The fire truck is ____ .

    a toy truck

    an imaginary truck

    a real truck

3. "Rescue" means "____ ."

    play with

    save

    buy

4. Which hat is the boy wearing?

C. **Answer the questions.**

1. What product is the ad promoting?

    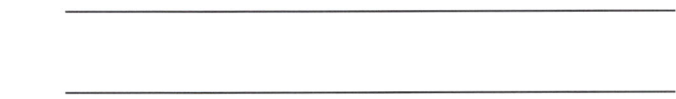

 An ad is a media text that can be used to promote a product to an audience – a group of people the ad is designed for.

2. Who do you think is the audience of this ad?

    _____

3. Why are some words in the ad in bold?

    _____

D. Look at the ad. Then circle and check the correct answers.

1. Product:
   superwoman costume / superwoman figurine

2. Intended Audience:
   parents / young boys / young girls

3. Purpose:
   to inform / to instruct / to persuade / to entertain

4. Slogan: **Be a Superwoman! / SALE**

5. Price: **$20.99 / $15.99**

6. Overt Message (clear, direct, and obvious message):

   Ⓐ Girls are superwomen.

   Ⓑ Superwomen love this costume.

7. Implied Message (hidden message):

   Ⓐ Superwomen can fly in this costume.

   Ⓑ You will be strong like a superwoman in this costume.

E. Fill in the information about an ad for a product. Then design the ad.

Product: _____

Features of Product: _____

Price: _____   Purpose of Ad: _____

Intended Audience: _____

Slogan: _____

Overt Message: _____

Implied Message: _____

My Ad

Words That I Have Learned

_____
_____
_____

Review 4 — Reading and Writing

A. Circle the answers.

1. A story has ____ .
   - characters
   - an instruction
   - rhyming words

2. Which group of words shows the sequence of events in a story?
   - because, after, then
   - before, after, then
   - and, or, but

3. ____ is a story passed on through speech.
   - An ad
   - A letter
   - A folktale

4. Whose name appears at the bottom of a letter?
   - the receiver's
   - the sender's
   - the mail carrier's

5. An envelope needs ____ .
   - a greeting
   - a picture
   - addresses and a stamp

6. In a rhyme, the stanzas are like ____ .
   - stories
   - paragraphs
   - poems

7. In the AABB rhyme scheme, the ____ and ____ lines rhyme.
   - first ; fourth
   - first ; third
   - first ; second

8. Which text type has rhyming words?
   - a diagram
   - a poem
   - a letter

9. A diagram is a type of ____ .

   literary text

   graphic text

   poem

10. A diagram has ____ .

    a compass and arrows

    labels and pictures

    text and a compass

11. Which is a recipe?

12. A recipe includes ____ .

    step-by-step instructions

    dates, numbers, and names

    a slogan and price

13. Which is not a characteristic of an informational text?

    contains headings

    contains facts

    contains fictional information

14. The facts in an informational text can be put under ____ .

    different legends

    different titles

    different subheadings

15. Which one is a media text?

    a rhyme

    an ad

    a recipe

B. Read the text. Then check if the sentences are true. Put a cross if they are false.

The Bumblebee

The bumblebee is an important insect. It is a very good pollinator, which means it helps spread pollen from one plant to another so that other plants can grow.

Physical Characteristics

A bumblebee is yellow and black and has six legs. It has two antennae for smelling, and a female bumblebee has a stinger for defending itself.

Habitat

Most bumblebees live in a nest. Each group or colony has a queen, worker bees, and drones. The queen bee is the leader. It lays four to eight eggs in the nest after a winter in hibernation. The eggs hatch to become worker bees, which are female, and drones, which are male. The colony grows until it has 50 to 600 bees.

Diet

A bumblebee uses the sweet nectar and pollen from flowers for energy. A worker bee makes honey by chewing the pollen and mixing it with its saliva.

1. The bumblebee is a good pollinator. ○
2. All bumblebees have a stinger. ○
3. Each colony has a queen, a king, and worker bees. ○
4. The queen bee lays four to eight eggs in the nest after hibernating. ○
5. A bumblebee uses the pollen from plants to make honey. ○

C. **Answer the questions.**

1. What type of text is this?

   _____

2. How does a bumblebee help plants grow?

   _____

3. How does a worker bee make honey?

   _____

   _____

4. Do you think the bumblebee is an important insect? Why or why not?

   _____

   _____

Review 4 — Reading and Writing

D. Label to complete the diagram of the life cycle of a bumblebee. Then write a short poem that follows a rhyme scheme about bumblebees.

adult   larva   egg

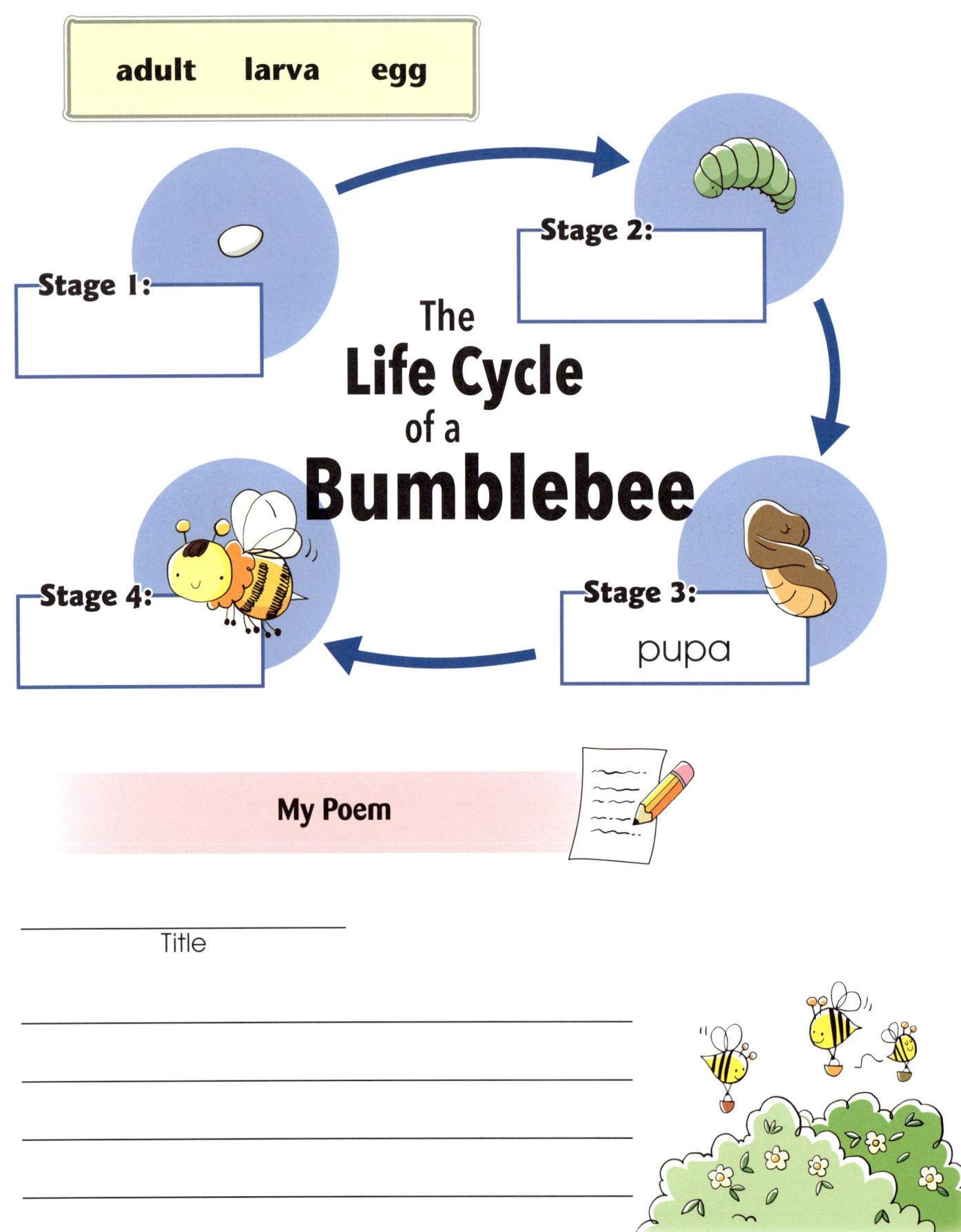

The Life Cycle of a Bumblebee

Stage 1:
Stage 2:
Stage 3: pupa
Stage 4:

My Poem

_____
Title

_____

_____

_____

_____

E. Fill in the information about an ad for a honey product. Then design the ad.

Product: _____

Product Features: _____

Purpose of Ad: _____

Intended Audience: _____

Slogan: _____

Overt Message: _____

Implied Message: _____

Price

Design your ad in the box below.

Answers

Answers

Section 1

1 Consonants

A. Beginning Consonant: (b)at ; (f)ish ; (d)uck

Middle Consonant: koa(l)a ; pe(t)al ; ba(n)a(n)a

Ending Consonant: bu(s) ; pe(n) ; ja(r)

B.

	Beginning Consonant		Middle Consonant		Ending Consonant	
	h	j	p	s	r	b
c r a b						✓
j a m		✓				
s t a r					✓	
h a t	✓					
m u s i c				✓		
h a m m e r	✓		✓			

C. Beginning Consonant:
queen ; mouse ; turtle ; nurse
Middle Consonant:
hockey ; beaver ; fairy
Ending Consonant:
STOP ; book

D. Alaska

Alaska is our largest and (n)ther(n)most state. It is (n)ear the (N)orth Pole so it is very cold there. Despite the cold weather, ma(n)y a(n)imals such as polar bears and moose call Alaska home.

I(n) Alaska, there are two mo(n)ths of dark(n)ess and two mo(n)ths of daylight. You might see the su(n) shi(n)ing at (n)i(n)e o'clock at (n)ight i(n) Ju(n)e, just like it does at (n)oo(n)!

2 Hard and Soft "c" and "g"

A. 1.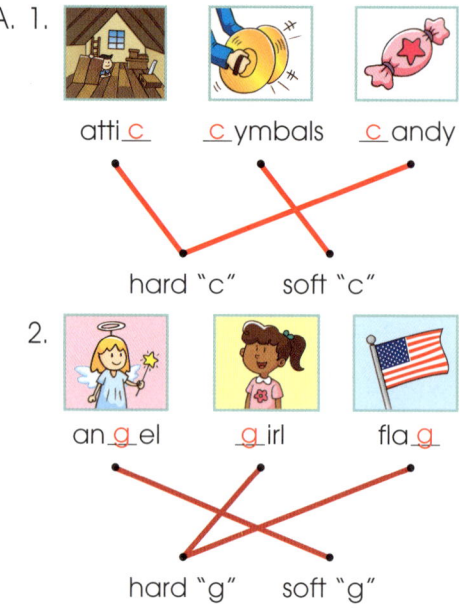

atti(c)   (c)ymbals   (c)andy

hard "c"   soft "c"

2. an(g)el   (g)irl   fla(g)

hard "g"   soft "g"

B. 1. Hard c: castle
   2. Hard g: gift
   3. Soft c: dancer
   4. Soft g: giraffe

C. Hard "c": cage, carrot, circus
Soft "c": juice, celery, circus
Hard "g": goose, bag, garbage
Soft "g": cage, garbage, danger, genie

D. Pen(g)uins

Pen(g)uins are birds that (c)annot fly but are (g)ood swimmers. They live in i(c)y Antar(c)ti(c)a and off the (c)oast of Afri(c)a and Australia. The smallest pen(g)uin is about 13 inches tall. It is (c)alled the blue pen(g)uin. The tallest pen(g)uin, the emperor, seems hu(g)e in (c)omparison!

The female pen(g)uin lays an e(gg) or two and (g)oes off in search of food. While she is (g)one, the male prote(c)ts the e(gg)s from dan(g)er.

Complete English Success (Grade 2)

Answers Section 1

3 Silent Consonants

A. 1. ta(l)k 2. sta(l)k
   3. crum(b) 4. (k)night
   5. spag(h)etti 6. clim(b)
   7. (k)not 8. anc(h)or

B.

C. 1. l 2. k
   3. h 4. b
   5. l

D. (h)onest ; ca(l)m ; (k)nock ; c(h)oir
   1. honest 2. Knock
   3. calm 4. choir

E. Kelvin the (Knight)

Kelvin was an (honorable) (knight). He was charged with capturing the thieving (ghosts) called Creepie and Spook. At first, Kelvin (thought) he (would) lure them with (crumbs) or (salmon), but he (knew) they were not that (dumb). Then he came up with another (scheme). He (knitted) a web and (calmly) waited for the (ghosts) to arrive. They got (caught) in his trap and Kelvin was declared the (heir) to the throne.

4 Consonant Blends: L Blends

A. 1. cl 2. bl
   3. bl 4. fl
   5. pl 6. fl
   7. sl 8. gl

B.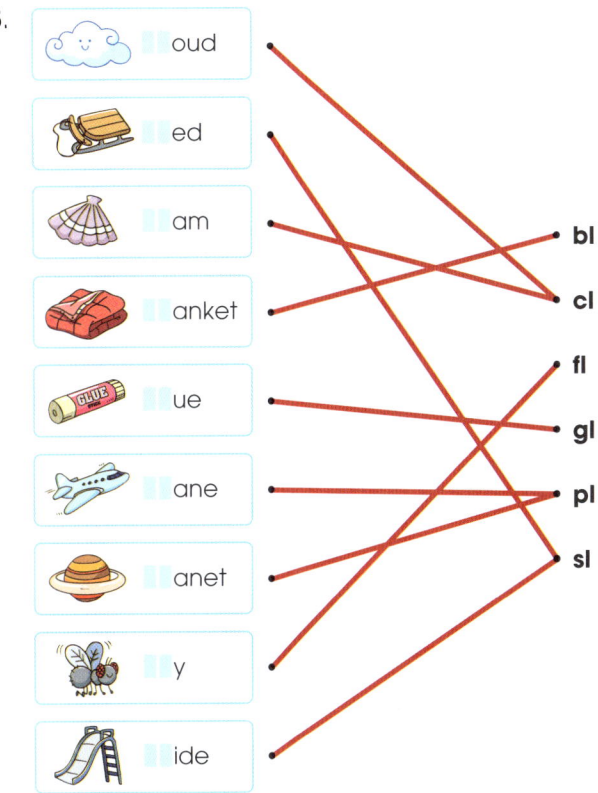

Complete English Success (Grade 2)

Answers

Section 1

C. 1. gl   2. fl
   3. pl   4. fl
   5. pl   6. Fl
   7. sl   8. sl
   9. bl ; cl

D. Ladybugs

Ladybugs are insects. They are often red with (black) spots. Some are (black) with red spots. In the summer, they live on (flowers), shrubs, and other (plants). In the winter, they live in trees and houses.

Ladybugs are capable of (flying). Although they cannot reach the (clouds), they can reach great heights. On land, they are small enough to crawl on (flowers) and even on tiny (blades) of grass.

5 Consonant Blends: R Blends

A. 1. cr   2. gr
   3. dr   4. fr
   5. br   6. tr
   7. p_r_ince
      t_r_ain
      t_r_ack

B. fr, (blank), gr, (blank), tr, cr, fr, pr, br, tr, (blank), dr

C. 1. ✔   2. ✘ ; bread
   3. ✘ ; crust   4. ✔
   5. ✘ ; brush   6. ✘ ; tray

D. (cr)ops ; (Fr)iday ; (tr)ip ; (pr)esident
   1. trip   2. crops
   3. Friday   4. president

E. (Trisha's) (Dream)

A few days ago, (Trisha) had a (dreadful) (dream). She was standing under some tall (trees) in a scary forest. She suddenly felt huge (drops) of rain on her (dress)! (Trisha) ran in the wet (grass) to hide inside a small (brick) house. It was then that she woke up to realize that, in reality, there was rain coming in (from) her window!

232 Complete English Success (Grade 2)

Answers — Section 1 — Grade 2

6 Consonant Blends: S Blends

A. 1. sc   2. sk
   3. sl   4. sm
   5. sn   6. sp
   7. st   8. sw

B.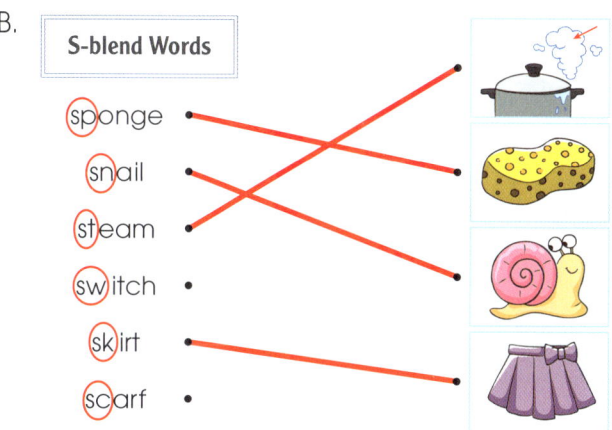
S-blend Words: (sp)onge, (sn)ail, (st)eam, (sw)itch, (sk)irt, (sc)arf

C. 1. sl   2. sl
   3. sm   4. sw
   5. sm   6. sk

D. 1.
snowman, spade, scarf

2. smoothie   3. smell
4. spot   5. stairs
6. swan   7. scooter
8. skip

E. Dance Lessons

When (Stella) was three years old, she (started) taking dance lessons. She wore a pink (skirt) with (small) ballet (slippers). She practiced the (steps) every day.

By the time she was 16, she was very good at ballet. (Stella) was offered the leading role in a play called "(Swan)." She quickly learned many new (steps) and routines. Because of her hard work, (Stella) (spun) in circles and (slowly) bowed as she became the (star) of the (stage)!

Complete English Success (Grade 2)

Answers Section 1

7 Consonant Digraphs

A. th ; ch ; wh ; sh ; sh ; sh

B. 1. th 2. sh
   3. wh 4. wh
   5. sh 6. th
   7. ch

C. 1. (Sh)e sells sea(sh)ells by (th)e sea(sh)ore.

   2. (Ch)ester (ch)ewed (th)e (ch)ewing gum (ch)eerily.

   3. (Th)e (sh)iny (sh)oes in Susie's (Sh)oe (Sh)op (sh)immer in (th)e (sh)ining sun.

   4. (Th)eodore (th)ought (th)e (th)imble was (th)ick.

   5. (Th)e (th)in (th)ief (th)rew (th)e (th)read to (th)e o(th)er (th)ree (th)ieves.

   6. Willy (th)e (Wh)ale (wh)irled (wh)ile (th)e (wh)eel of (th)e (wh)ite (wh)aler (wh)istled.

D. (Individual examples)

 sh    wh

 ch    th

E. Sheila's Shopping Adventure

Sheila was excited to go shopping with her elder brother, Chandler. She woke up early on Thursday and showered quickly. Then she threw on her favorite pink dress with white shoes. She was going to buy things for everyone: shampoo for her dog, red thread with a shiny thistle for her grandma, delicious cherries for her mom, and a whistle to surprise Chandler.

However, once they started the car, they noticed that its steering wheel was not working. So they took the bus instead. Sheila saw a big cheese factory, a giant chair, and a whale museum on her way to the mall!

8 Short Vowels

A. 1. n(e)t   2. l(a)mp
   3. t(e)nt   4. s(i)x
   5. b(u)g   6. m(a)p
   7. m(o)p   8. s(u)n
   9. l(i)ps   10. r(o)ck

B. 1.

   2.

   3.

   4.

   5.

C. 1. i   2. o
   3. e   4. a
   5. u

D. 1. e   2. a
   3. u   4. o
   5. i

234 Complete English Success (Grade 2)

Answers Section 1 Grade 2

E. Jill's Umbrella Hat

(Jill) has an umbrella (hat). It is an umbrella, (but) it is also a hat. It was a (gift) from her (mom). She (can) use it in the rain and also in the (sun). She (wears) it on her (head). (Ron) likes her umbrella hat too. He thinks it is (fun) to wear it.

9 Long Vowels

A. 1. i   2. o
   3. a   4. i
   5. e   6. u
   7. a   8. u

B. 1.

2.

3.

4.

5.

C.

Long-vowel Words

sp(i)der
r(u)ler
wh(a)le
gl(o)be
(a)corn
f(i)re
z(e)bra
m(u)sic
(e)vent
(o)cean

D. All about Plants

(Most) plants start as seeds. (Usually), (you) plant the seed in the garden or the yard, in the (shade) or the sun.

If (you) (use) a small (spade), (you) can dig a (hole) to (poke) the seed down and cover it with soil. Plant the seed and let the sun shine down on it. When it sprouts and the stem gets stronger, leaves begin to come out.

Answers

Section 1

10 Y as a Vowel

A. 1. i   2. e
    3. e   4. e
    5. e   6. i
    7. i   8. i

B. fairy — Y as Long "e"
    puppy — Y as Long "e"
    butterfly — Y as Long "e"
    sky — Y as Long "i"
    family — Y as Long "e"
    July — Y as Long "i"

C. Y as Long "i" (in red): my ; try ; fly ; dry ; fry
    Y as Long "e" (in blue): funny ; buddy ; sunny ; pony ; Mary

    1. Mary   2. funny
    3. Buddy   4. dry
    5. try   6. sunny
    7. fly   8. my
    9. fry   10. pony

D. The Coin Collection

<u>Brittany</u> has a coin collection. She started it when she was six years old. She put the coins in a jar labeled "(My) Coins." The first coins she got were from <u>Italy</u>, which her mom gave her after a trip there. Since then, <u>many</u> of her <u>family</u> members have given her coins for gifts. Her dad will (fly) to China in (July) and he will (try) to find some special coins for her. <u>Brittany's</u> favorite coin is one from Sri Lanka. It is large and <u>heavy</u>.

11 Vowel Digraphs

A.

- I love to swim in the s<u>ea</u>.
- tr<u>ee</u>
- p<u>ai</u>l
- ch<u>ai</u>r
- I f<u>ee</u>l so happy on my holid<u>ay</u>.
- b<u>ea</u>ch

B. 1. nail   2. snail
    3. tray   4. jay
    5. pay   6. say
    7. paint   8. play
    9. jail

C. 1. bee   2. jeans
    3. tea   4. team
    5. bean   6. meat
    7. weed   8. week
    9. see   10. seed

D. (Individual answers)

Answers

Section 1   Grade 2

E. Adventure at the (Sea)
(Dear) (Jayden),
We went to Sharaz on (Thursday). On our (way), we heard about a sunken ship in the (deep) (sea). The story goes like this – a pirate ship got caught in the (rain) there a long time ago. It sank and a chest with precious gems and gold (beads) went down with it.

At first, we were (afraid) of the water, but then we decided to look for the ship. We boarded a small ship. Then we dived under the water. When we (reached) the ship, we swam inside and guess what? We found the chest!

I'll show you some photos when we're home.

Your friend,
(Dean)

12 Vowel Digraph: oo

A. 1. 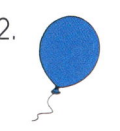   2.    3.

4.    5.    6.

7.

B. Long oo: smoothie, roots, boot, noodles, zoo
Short oo: brook, hood, foot
(Individual examples)

C. 1. short ; long
   2. cook ; book ; look ; cookbook
   3. fool ; pool ; cool ; drool

D. Noor's Smoothie Recipe

Noor was a very (good) (cook). But she did not want to make the same food every day. So she (stood) in the kitchen and (looked) around. Finally, she decided to put some apples, strawberries, bananas, and three scoops of chocolate ice cream into the blender. She pushed the red button and "whoosh" it went as it (shook) the small (wooden) table. She excitedly poured the mixture into her glass. Noor hummed in a (good) mood as she drank the delicious smoothie.

Complete English Success (Grade 2)   237

Answers

Section 1

13 Diphthongs

A. 1. ou 2. oi
   3. ou 4. ow
   5. oy 6. oy
   7. oi 8. ow

B. 1. oy ; royal   2. oi ; noise
   3. ow ; town   4. ou ; mouth

C. ou: trout, found, shout, out
   ow: shower, towel, down
   oi: boil, coin, voice, avoid
   oy: voyage, loyal, employ, joy

D. R(oy) the T(oy) Robot

   R(oy) was very ann(oy)ed with his sister, J(oy). She was ar(ou)nd two years old and enj(oy)ed destr(oy)ing his things. She even sp(oi)led his favorite drawing of blue cl(ou)ds over a sea of tr(ou)t and the one with a cr(ow)d of silly cl(ow)ns. At first, R(oy) yelled at her in a l(ou)d v(oi)ce. Then he heard her cry on the c(ou)ch. So he decided to surprise her. He took a piece of f(oi)l, some br(ow)n paper, and a metal c(oi)l. After a lot of hard work, "R(oy) the T(oy) Robot" went to his sister and they played together until their mother was back home.

B. 1. book ; ~~door~~
   2. duck ; ~~quack~~
   3. cake ; ~~cage~~
   4. frog ; ~~wok~~
   5. sun ; ~~mom~~
   6. plane ; ~~man~~

C.

D. (Circle each pair or group of rhyming words with the same color.)
   Rhyming pairs/groups:
   deep – sheep – deep – sleep
   cat – rat
   bear – hare – pear
   dog – frog
   moose – goose

14 Rhyming Words

A. (Color each rhyming pair with the same color.)
   cap – map
   tea – tree
   knot – pot
   tub – cub

Answers

Section 1 — Grade 2

Review 1

A. 1. middle
    2.
    3. knife
    4. cl
    5.
    6. s
    7. wheel, thumb, chair
    8. short vowel
    9. long "a"
    10.
    11. ai
    12. hook
    13.
    14. diphthong
    15. bite, sight
    16.

B.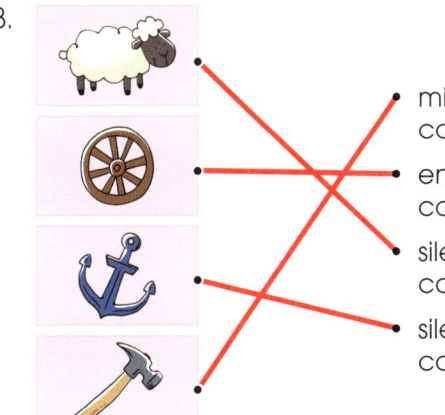

C. 1. The (g)i(g)anti(c) (g)iant, (G)ary, used ma(g)i(c) to de(c)orate the (c)astle.
   2. There were (c)akes and (c)andies in the (g)arden on (C)arl's birthday.
   3. The dan(c)ers (c)elebrated as Andy played the (g)uitar.

D. 1. cl   2. dr
   3. st   4. fr
   5. sk   6. fl

E. 1.    2.
   3.    4.

F. Short Vowel: a ; u
   Long Vowel: i ; o
   (Individual examples)

G.
	Short-vowel Word	Long-vowel Word
1.	Bill	grapes
2.	pink	slide
3.	mat	rose
4.	pet	bone
5.	rocks	night

H. 1. ee ; ee   2. ai ; ea
   3. ai ; ay   4. oo ; oo

I. ou: clouds, outside
   ow: crown, brown
   oi: soil, noise
   oy: boy, annoying

Complete English Success (Grade 2)

Answers Section 2

1 Nouns

A. Person: boy ; Timmy
   Animal: dog ; Dalmatian
   Place: city ; Seattle
   Thing: game ; Frisbee

B. 1. parrot   2. fairy
   3. foxes   4. dresses
   5. brushes   6. chicks
   7. bench   8. rat
   9. kids

C.
   carrot**s**   jam____   popcorn____
   glass **es**   ball**s**   cheese____

D. 1. water ; cups
   2. bottles ; plastic
   3. sand ; pots
   4. faith ; heroes

E. Countable Noun: farm , market, cows , animals, hens, eggs, sheep
   Uncountable Noun: soil, dirt, air, water, wool, milk

2 Articles

A. a: house, uniform, violin
   an: apricot, umbrella, idea, album
   the: South Pole, White House, NYPD, Colorado River
   (Individual examples)

B. 1. the sun
   2. an owl
   3. an elephant
   4. a rainbow ; a unicorn
   5. a lamp
   6. the North Pole
   7. the moon
   8. an airplane

C. 1. the   2. an ; a
   3. the ; the   4. The
   5. the ; the ; a 6. the ; an
   7. A   8. an
   9. a ; the   10. the

D. (Individual writing)

3 Pronouns

A.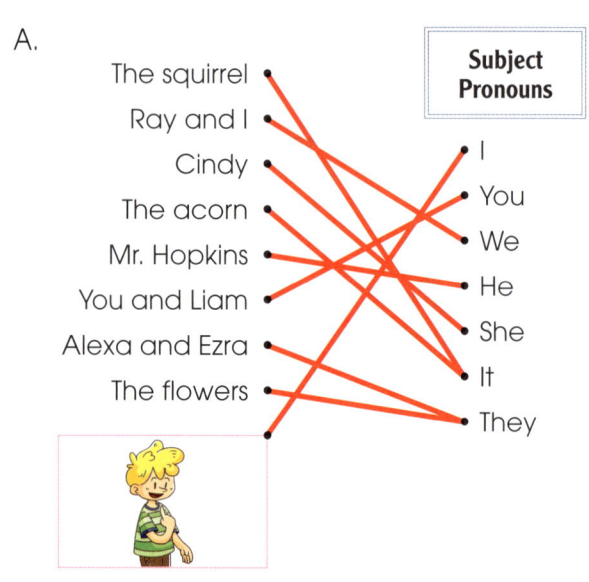

B. 1. We   2. They
   3. She   4. It
   5. I

C. They ; We ; He ; It

D. 1. you   2. it
   3. them ; me   4. him
   5. us ; her

E. 1. her   2. them
   3. us   4. you
   5. him   6. us
   7. it   8. him ; them

F. 1. us   2. it
   3. them   4. him
   5. us   6. her

Answers Section 2 Grade 2

4 Present Tense Verbs

A. 1. sing ; singing
    2. laughs ; laughing
    3. break ; breaking
    4. leap ; leaps
    5. snows ; snowing
    6. find ; finding

B. 1. shines
    2. walking
    3. chat
    4. live
    5. waving
    6. looking

C. 1. eat   2. gets
    3. stay   4. blowing
    5. plays   6. collecting

D. 1. are   2. are
    3. is   4. is
    5. is   6. are
    7. are   8. are ; am

E. A. I am reading a letter.
    B. The calves are playing happily.
    C. Gavin is swinging in the tree.

5 Past Tense Verbs

A.
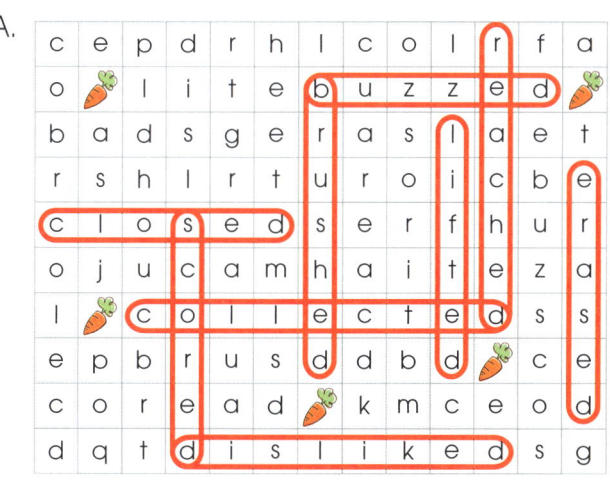

B. Dodo carryed / **carried** a backpack to school yesterday. He learnd / **learned** some funny tricks at the dog school. He **balanced** / balanceed himself with one hand on a plank on a ball. After that, he skiped / **skipped** for an hour. Then he hurryed / **hurried** home for lunch. On his way home, he **remembered** / rememberred that there was no more dog food at home, so he stoped / **stopped** by a grocery store and grabed / **grabbed** some dog food. He also tryed / **tried** to look for a bone as a treat, but he could not find one that he **liked** / likeed.

C. 1. stood   2. caught
    3. burst   4. bought
    5. wept   6. threw
    7. taught   8. spread

D. 1. was   2. ✔
    3. ✔   4. were

6 Adjectives

A.
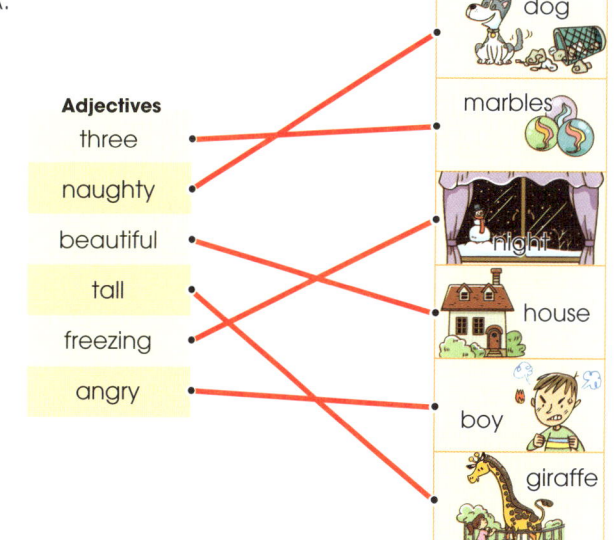

B. 1. apple   2. cat
    3. diamond   4. sweater
    5. candy   6. book
    7. tree   8. girl
    9. castle   10. ball

Complete English Success (Grade 2)

Section 2

C. 1. Green 2. juicy
   3. seven 4. round
   5. spicy 6. new ; yellow
   7. black ; white ; fresh 8. puzzled
   9. lazy

D. 1. big 2. pretty
   3. six 4. scary
   5. red
   (Individual writing)

7 Prepositions

A. 1. in 2. behind
   3. over 4. on ; by
   5. between 6. at ; in

B. Samuel is <u>under</u> ⟨on⟩ a cruise ship. He is sitting <u>at</u> ✔ a table <u>in</u> ⟨on⟩ the deck enjoying the cool breeze. There are some clouds <u>over</u> ⟨in⟩ the sky, but the weather is still fine. There is a drink <u>under</u> ⟨on⟩ the table. Samuel does not know what is <u>in</u> ✔ the glass, but he thinks it tastes amazing. A little bird is <u>in front of</u> ⟨behind⟩ Samuel. It seems to want to share the tranquil moment with him. The cruise ship is not too far <u>on</u> ⟨from⟩ the shore. Samuel can see people that look as tiny as ants <u>between</u> ⟨on⟩ the beach.

C. 1. on 2. in
   3. at 4. in
   5. on 6. on
   7. at 8. on

D. Disney World

Disney World is an adventure park (in) Orlando, Florida. There are many Disney characters (in) the park. You can also see them (in) different parades that happen (at) different times (during) the day.

Disney World is an exciting place to visit. You can go there early (in) the morning and enjoy the whole day there. You can go on the many rides (around) the park. You can also try different types of foods (in) a variety of restaurants and (at) food kiosks. One of the most special moments to enjoy is the spectacular fireworks show that happens every day (at) sundown.

Disney World is known as the happiest place (on) Earth! Why not go there (on) a weekend or (in) the summer and enjoy the place where dreams come true?

8 Joining Words

A. 1. and 2. but
   3. and 4. or
   5. and ; or ; and 6. but
   7. or 8. but ; and
   9. but

B. 1. or 2. and
   3. but 4. but
   5. and ; or ; But ; and

C. 1. ✔
   2. Do you want to be a chef ~~or~~ and work in a restaurant?
   3. ✔

Answers   Section 2   Grade 2

4. I have to practice hard ~~but~~ [and] be better at dancing.
5. My brother only has one day off in a week. It is Saturday ~~and~~ [or] Sunday.

D. 1. My sister brushed her hair and she put on her favorite dress.
2. I wanted to show my picture to you, but it got ruined in the rain.
3. Rehearse more or you will not remember the lines.

E. Playing Soccer

Today I started soccer. My twin brother, Michael, [and] I went to a big field. There were lots of children, [but] none were beginners like us. Some of them were practicing their skills [and] others were playing a game.

The coach told us to pick an orange uniform, [or] a green one. I liked the green uniform, [and/but] Michael liked the orange one. Our coach was very nice [and] friendly. She told us that we would practice once a week, either on Saturday [or] Sunday. She said that the most important thing was to have fun.

9 The Sentence: Subject and Predicate

A. (Check these boxes.)
1. Period
2. Capital Letter ; Period
3. Period
4. Capital Letter
5. Capital Letter ; Period
6. Capital Letter
7. Capital Letter
8. Capital Letter ; Period
9. Period

B. 1. Mrs. Maddison
2. Brad's father
3. The birthday cake
4. Nina
5. The children
6. Brad's parents
7. The children
8. They
9. Brad
10. Andy
11. The party

C. 1. E
2. F
3. B
4. C
5. A
6. G
7. D
8. H

D. (Individual answers)

10 Subjects and Objects

A. 1. The girl
2. The hungry lion
3. The hamburger on the plate
4. My mom and dad
5. The book on the shelf
6. She
7. Ted and his sister
8. The cute kitten
9. That boy over there
10. Kayla, Miles, and I
11. The busy beaver

B. 1. all flavors of ice cream
2. the vase by the window
3. ✗
4. an apple pie
5. a warm jacket
6. computer games
7. ✗
8. ✗
9. all the soup in the big bowl
10. Samuel and me

C. 1. Allen the Chipmunk ; S
2. The trees in the forest ; S
3. food and shelter ; O
4. nuts and seeds ; O
5. fresh fruit ; O
6. tall trees ; O
7. various fun games ; O
8. Their parents ; S

Answers Section 2

9. Allen and his friends ; O
10. one another ; O
11. different sounds ; O

D. (Individual writing)

11 Types of Sentences

A. A: . B: .
   C: ? D: .
   E: ? F: ?
   G: ? H: .
   Telling Sentence: A, B, D, H
   Asking Sentence: C, E, F, G

B. 1. The news is on at nine o'clock.
   2. It snows in the winter.
   3. This vase is made of glass.
   4. They are sitting at the table.

C. 1. When — is that building?
   2. Why — can't penguins fly?
   3. What — is your birthday?
   4. Did — you solve the puzzle?
   5. Who — has left the scarf here?
   6. How tall — is under the chair?

D. 1. Exclamatory Sentence
   2. Imperative Sentence
   3. Imperative Sentence
   4. Exclamatory Sentence
   5. Imperative Sentence
   6. Exclamatory Sentence
   7. Imperative Sentence
   8. Imperative Sentence
   9. Exclamatory Sentence
   10. Exclamatory Sentence

E. (Individual writing)

12 Punctuation and Capitalization

A. 1. !   2. .
   3. ?   4. .
   5. .   6. ?
   7. .   8. !
   9. !

B. 1. !   2. ?
   3. !   4. .
   5. ?   6. !
   7. ?   8. !
   9. .

C. 1. !
   2. ✓
   3. ?
   4. !
   5. ✓
   6. !

D. beauty and the beast
   The Prince and the Pauper
   The Emperor's New Clothes
   Jack and the Beanstalk
   Goldilocks and the Three Bears
   anne of green gables

E. 1. Last year's Halloween was a Friday.
   2. Was Mrs. Jevon at home on New Year's Day?
   3. Jennifer, Ray, and I loved our picnic lunch!
   4. The concert was held in Chicago last August.
   5. "We Are the World" is such a great song!

Answers Section 2 Grade 2

13 Forming Negative Sentences

A. 1. ✔
   2. ✘
   3. ✔
   4. ✔
   5. ✔
   6. ✘

B. 1. Dad was **not** using the computer earlier.
   2. Zoey and Dennis were **not** at the party last night.
   3. They were **not** singing when the bell rang.
   4. Jacky was **not** waiting for the bus at two o'clock yesterday.
   5. We were **not** looking when the clown came out.
   6. Rachel and Percy were **not** classmates last year.
   7. The cherry pie we had this morning was **not** very delicious.
   8. Rhonda was **not** at home when Jane called.
   9. Sophia noticed that the machines were **not** functioning well.

C. 1. does not stop
   2. does not go
   3. do not grow
   4. does not sleep
   5. do not know
   6. do not want
   7. do not like

D. 1. Mom did not go to work last Saturday.
   2. I did not study in this school last year.
   3. Macy and Samuel did not play in the pool yesterday.
   4. Jason did not play video games last night.

14 Contractions

A. 1. he's   2. they're
   3. what's   4. I've
   5. there's   6. how's
   7. don't   8. they'll
   9. you've   10. doesn't
   11. didn't   12. shouldn't

B. 1. I ~~wasn't~~ **wasn't** sure how I broke the toy.
   2. ~~Where is~~ **Where's** the box office?
   3. ~~Isn't~~ **Isn't** this your lunch bag?
   4. ✔
   5. Katie ~~can't~~ **can't** finish the whole pizza.
   6. ✔
   7. ~~How is~~ **How's** everyone doing?
   8. ✔
   9. There ~~aren't~~ **aren't** any cookies left.
   10. ~~I am~~ **I'm** happy to have you as my friend.

C. (Circle these words.)
   couldn't ; here's ; she's ; we'd ; weren't ; hasn't ; they'll ; why's
   1. She's ; hasn't
   2. Here's
   3. weren't
   4. We'd
   5. They'll
   6. couldn't
   7. Why's

D. 1. It's chasing a rat.
   2. We'll have fun at the pool.
   3. That's the book I told you about.
   4. Let's take a rest under the tree.
   5. The children mustn't swim in the lake when no adults are around.

Complete English Success (Grade 2)   245

Answers

Section 2

Review 2

A. 1. City 2. boxes
   3. The girls are eating honey.
   4. the sun   5. We
   6. The boy is playing.   7. round
   8. behind   9. in
   10. Are you staying or leaving today?
   11. Ada loves animals.
   12. We rock!   13. . or !
   14. I do not like singing.

B. Common Noun: kingdom ; king ; elf
   Proper Noun: Colorland ; King Edwin ; Coby

C. Then someone said, "Look what (we) have found! It is a note left for (us) by Coby."

   To get all the colors back, Princess Lilian and Prince Ned have to search for one thing in each color. When (they) have found (it), (he) or (she) needs to touch (it) and say its color! Then that color will return to the kingdom. (I) will be hiding somewhere nearby to make sure (they) follow the rules.
   Coby

D. King Edwin carefully **studyied** / (**studied**) Coby's note. Then he said, "My children (are) / am very brave. I am allow / (am allowing) them to begin the search today!"
   The king asked Wilkin to accompany the children. Wilkin had an idea, "We (are going) / is going to look all over the woods just outside Colorland before we (go) / went any farther."

E. 1. between ; and
   2. under ; and
   3. on

F. 1. Lilian
   2. Ned
   3. (Individual answer)
   4. (Individual answer)

G. (The children) gathered some fruits. (They) ate the oranges, peaches, and grapes. (Lilian) said, "(I) love fruits! But (I) am worried. How are (we) going to find yellow?"
   "Look!" said (Ned). (They) saw some roses. "Maybe (they) are yellow."
   "But (roses) can be pink, red, or white, too," said (Wilkin).
   "(That) reminds me! (We) have to find red as well!" (Lilian) said in a panic.

H. B
   A
   C
   D

I. ~~a~~^After they had found the color red, the children retrieved the color yellow with a sunflower and returned to ~~c~~^Colorland (.).
   "~~l~~^Let's celebrate (!)" cheered the people (.).
   "~~h~~^How have you been (?)" asked ~~k~~^King ~~e~~^Edwin (.).
   "~~w~~^We are good (.) ~~w~~^We had fun (!)" replied ~~n~~^Ned (.).
   "~~l~~^Look (,)" said ~~l~~^Lilian as they saw ~~c~~^Coby disappear into thin air (.). ~~h~~^He had left behind a book titled ~~m~~^Magic ~~s~~^Spells (.).

Complete English Success (Grade 2)

Answers Section 3 Grade 2

1 Sense Words

A. 1. see ; eyes
   2. smell ; nose
   3. hear ; ears
   4. touch ; hands
   5. taste ; tongue

B.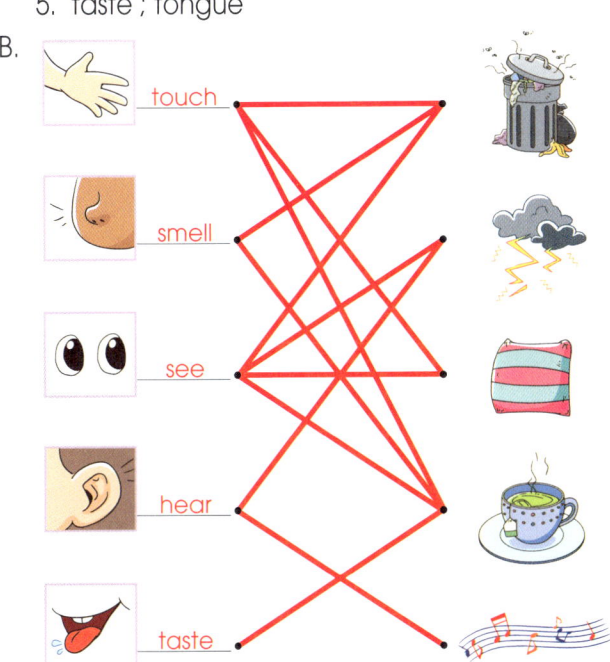

C. 1. hot   2. sharp
   3. fluffy   4. soft
   5. cold   6. hard
   7. rough   8. smooth
   9. sticky

D. (Individual drawings)
   1. sour   2. salty
   3. spicy   4. sweet
   5. bitter

2 Season Words

A. 1. spring   2. summer
   3. fall   4. winter

B. 1. warmer ; rainy
   2. cold ; snowy
   3. cool ; breezy
   4. hot ; sunny

C.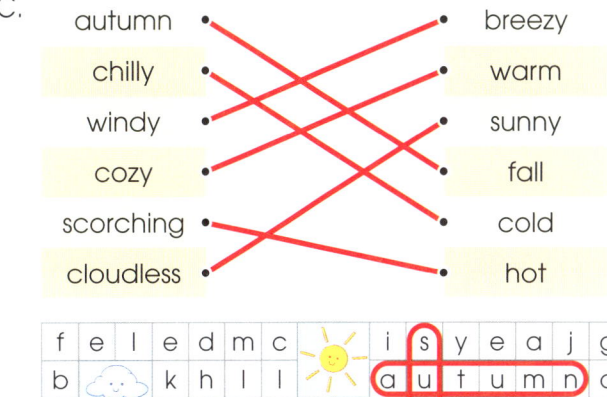

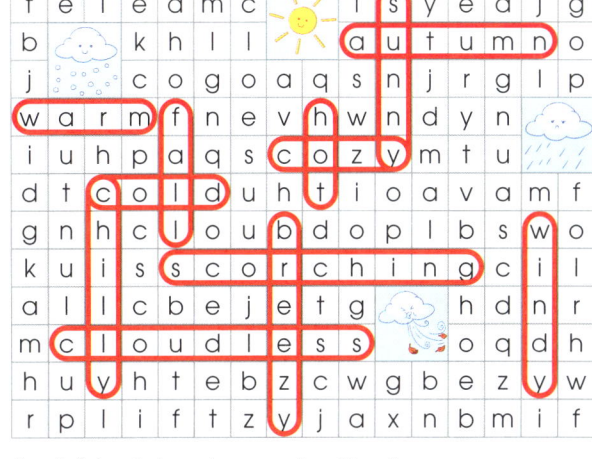

D. (Individual drawing and writing)

3 Camping Words

A. A: rope
   B: sleeping bag
   C: flashlight

B.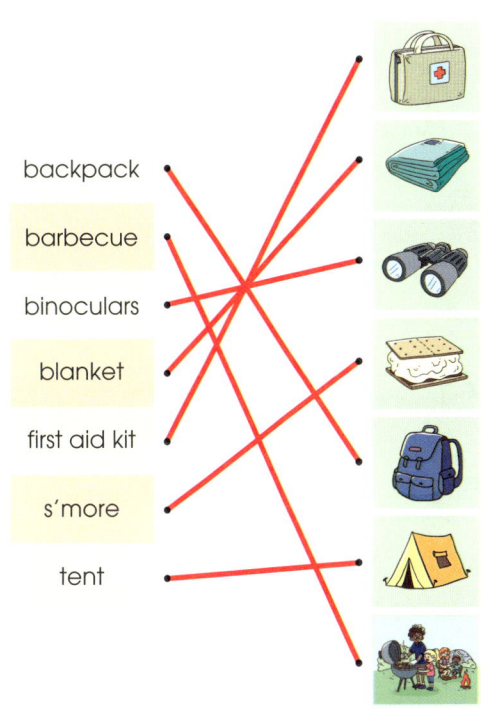

Complete English Success (Grade 2)

Answers Section 3

C. 1. marshmallow   2. charcoal
   3. compass   4. matches
   5. boots   6. clothespin
   7. flask   8. ax
   9. sunscreen   10. lantern

D. 1. stargazing
   2. Wildlife watching
   3. hiking
   4. Canoeing

4 Community Words

A. 1. townhouse   2. apartment building
   3. bungalow

B. A: library   B: school
   C: swimming pool D: fire station
   E: park   F: apartment building
   G: townhouse   H: police station
   I: hospital   J: supermarket
   K: bakery
   Q ; L ; O ; P ; M ; N

C.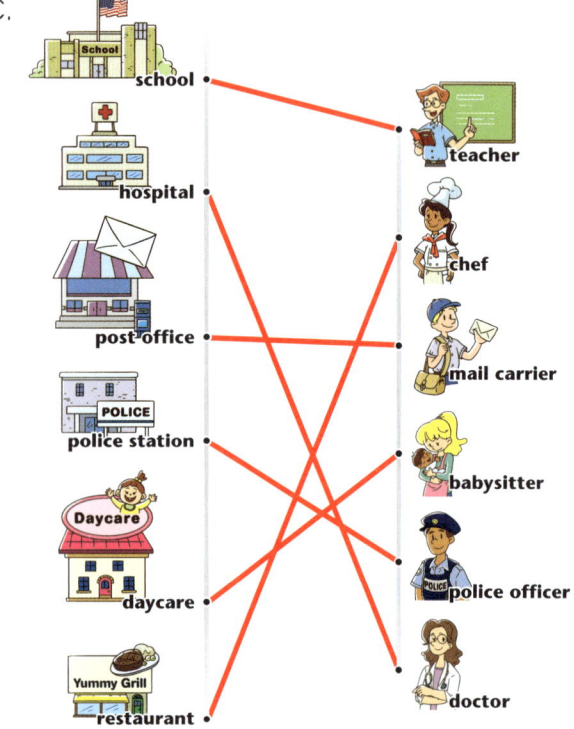

D. 1. chef   2. doctor
   3. convenience store 4. theater
   5. mail carrier   6. library

5 Polygon Words

A. 1. hexagon
   2. circle
   3. quadrilateral

B. 1. A   2. C
   3. C   4. A
   5. C   6. C ; A

C. (Individual tracing)
   1. 8 sides ; octagon
   2. 5 sides ; pentagon
   3. 3 sides ; triangle
   4. 4 sides ; quadrilateral
   5. 6 sides ; hexagon

D. (Suggested drawings)

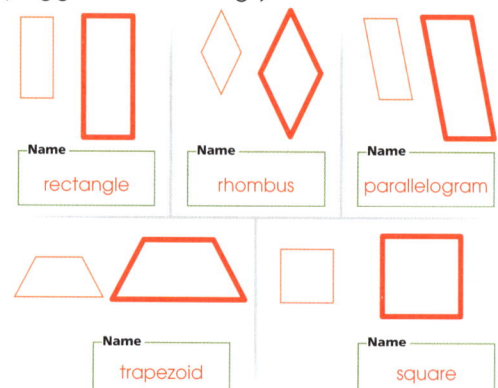

6 Computer Words

A. 1. monitor
   2. screen
   3. modem

B.

I can listen to music with my **headphones**.

Complete English Success (Grade 2)

Answers Section 3 Grade 2

C.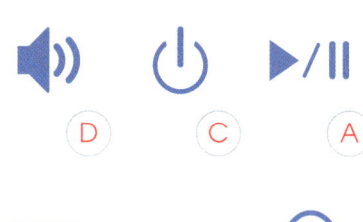

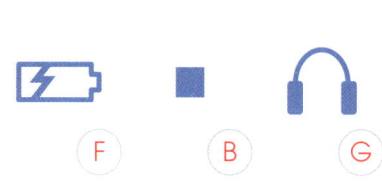

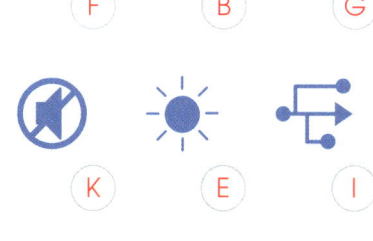

D. 1. music 2. information
3. buy 4. communicate
5. photos

D.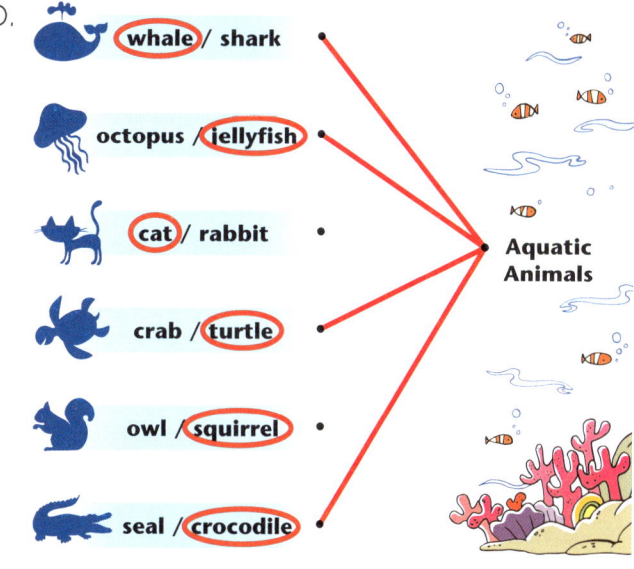

7 Water Words

A. 1. sea 2. pond
3. brook 4. stream
5. lake 6. creek
7. river 8. ocean

B. C ; A ; D ; B ; E
1. Pacific Ocean
2. Arctic Ocean
3. Indian Ocean
4. Southern Ocean
5. Atlantic Ocean

C. 1. geyser 2. delta
3. glacier 4. reservoir
5. waterfall 6. swamp
7. fjord

8 Synonyms

A. tasty: delicious ; yummy
sad: unhappy
pretty: beautiful
big: large
happy: glad
Mom: mother
picked: chose

B. 1. frightened 2. shiny
3. tiny 4. drowsy
5. hungry

C. 1. buddy ; pal
2. leap ; hop
3. furious ; mad
4. smart ; intelligent
5. courageous ; bold

D. 1. crying 2. breezy
3. tired 4. little
5. damp 6. store
7. hard 8. fast
9. dirty 10. huge

E. 1. Little Ryan loves the fluffy bunny.
2. Please shut the door behind you.
3. Did you hear that weird noise?
4. Hana's performance was awesome.
5. Let's fill the pails with water.

Complete English Success (Grade 2)   249

Answers Section 3

9 Antonyms

A. (Color each pair of antonyms with the same color.)
   hot – cold
   thick – thin
   wet – dry
   day – night
   short – long
   less – more

B. (Cross out these words.)
   1. messy
   2. provide
   3. afraid
   4. open
   5. large
   6. plain

C. C ; A ; D ; E ; B

D. stay: go, depart, leave
   wrong: correct, right, proper
   sad: glad, happy, jolly
   slow: fast, swift, speedy
   easy: difficult, hard, challenging

E. (Circle these words.)
   1. early – late
   2. best – worst ; calm – windy
   3. opened – closed ; went – came ; up – down

   1. early ; late
   2. best ; worst
      calm ; windy
   3. opened ; closed
      went ; came
      up ; down

10 Homophones

A. 1. rode   2. too
   3. blew   4. sun
   5. tale   6. sea
   7. knight   8. deer

B.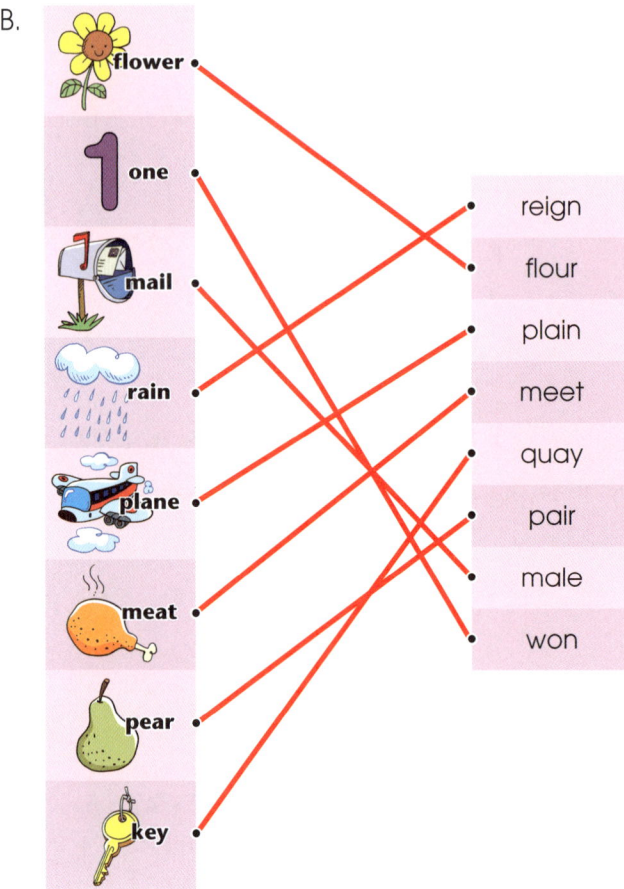

C. 1. bear   2. ate
   3. by   4. cents
   5. weight   6. knew
   7. hear   8. some
   9. flower   10. sell
   11. bee   12. write

D. 1. Kelly taught us how to tie a knot.
   2. I picked berries on my way to Grandma's house.
   3. Ricky played basketball for an hour.
   4. The hare hopped away when we got closer.

Answers

Review 3

A.
1. sight
2. winter
3. compass
4. flask
5. in a bakery
6. pentagon
7. volume control
8. a computer word
9. a glacier
10. a geyser
11. drowsy
12. neighbor
13. brave
14. leave
15. our
16. wait

B. Sense Word: see, hear, sweet, salty, smooth
Season Word: fall, chilly, autumn, windy, cozy, cloudless
Camping Word: camping, boots, tent, backpacks, canoeing, campsite, s'mores, barbecued, campfire, binoculars, stargazing

C.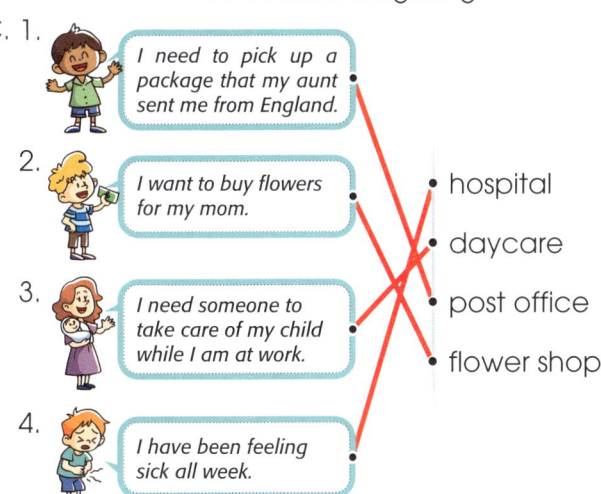

D.
1. rhombus
2. octagon
3. A: pentagon
   B: rectangle
   C: triangle

E.
1. monitor
2. CPU
3. keyboard
4. mouse

F.
1. river
2. delta
3. waterfall
4. pond
5. turtle

G.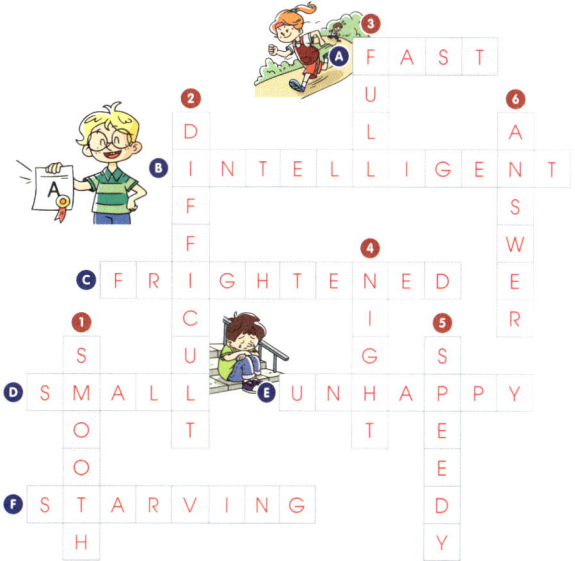

Answers Section 4

1 A Balloon Ride

A.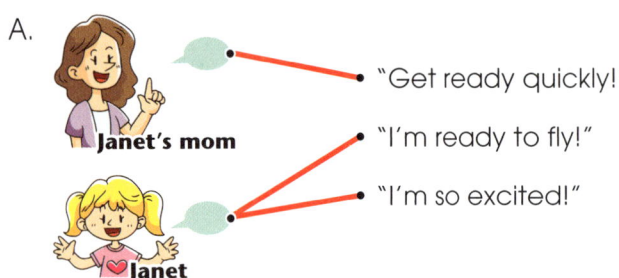
- "Get ready quickly!"
- "I'm ready to fly!"
- "I'm so excited!"

B. 1. excited
   2.
   3. her mom
   4. trees

C. 1. The setting is the park in the morning.
   2. The big adventure is a hot-air balloon ride.
   3. The hot-air balloon is colorful.

D. 1. A Balloon Ride
   2. Janet ; Janet's mom ; the man controlling the hot-air balloon
   3.
   4. morning

E. There is a burner in the hot-air balloon. The burner has to be lit. ~~You can light candles with matches.~~ It heats up the air in the balloon. ~~The children played a ball game.~~ The hot air makes the balloon rise into the sky.

F. (Cross out these sentences.)
   B: She had a nightmare.
   F: Some birds have wings but cannot fly.
   Janet got up early. Then she got ready and went to the park. Before the man lit the burner, Janet jumped into the basket. After the balloon lifted off, Janet felt like a bird flying.

2 The Sun and the Ocean

A. 1. ✔
   2. ✘
   3. ✘
   4. ✔
   5. ✘

B. 1. Grandpa's grandma
   2. friends
   3. the Ocean
   4. the Sun ; the Ocean

C. 1. Yes, it is a folktale.
   2. The rain falls to the earth.
   3. He turns into rain when he misses his home.

D.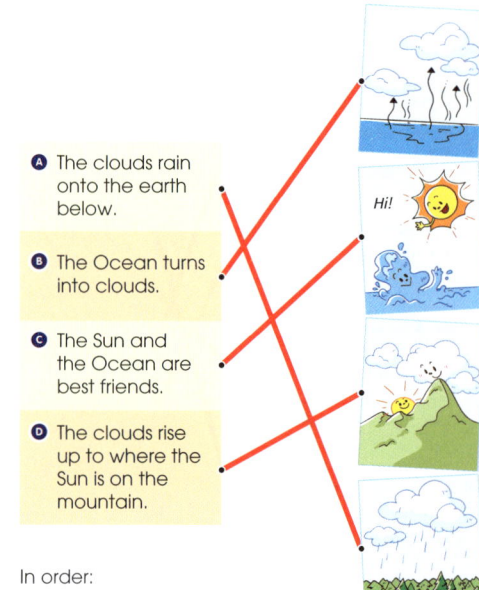

- A The clouds rain onto the earth below.
- B The Ocean turns into clouds.
- C The Sun and the Ocean are best friends.
- D The clouds rise up to where the Sun is on the mountain.

In order:
C ➡ B ➡ D ➡ A

E. The rain falls down to the earth. The Ocean becomes himself again. Then the Sun wants to visit the Ocean. He sets at dusk to meet his friend. The next morning, the Sun leaves his friend. He rises high up in the sky again.
(Individual drawing)

Answers — Section 4 — Grade 2

3 The Museum Trip

A. 1. a blue whale
   2. dinosaurs
   3. Earth and space
B. 1. a museum
   2. his classmates
   3. to the AMNH
   4.
C. 1. Todd ; Aunt Meg
   2. The full name of the AMNH is the American Museum of Natural History.
   3. Todd draws and writes about what he saw in the museum.
D. (Individual writing and drawing)
E. (Individual writing and drawing)

4 Alphabet Rhyme

A. 1. hive
   2. oar
   3. lamb
B. 1. eight
   2. 16
   3. kin
   4.
C. 1. It is a rhyme.
   2. There are four stanzas.
   3. bike – dike ; ear – gear ; five – hive ; inn – kin ; jam – lamb ; more – oar ; net – pet
D. (Individual drawings)
   Q
   road
   sail/sale
   T
E. (Individual writing)

5 Today Is My Birthday!

A. (Suggested drawing)

B. 1. today   2. seven years old
   3. the writer's friends   4. Mother
C. 1. It is his birthday.
   2. They will sing, eat, play, and run.
   3. hooray – birthday ; bake – cake ; sing – king ; run – fun
D. (Color these boxes.)
   This poem has a title.
   This poem has rhyming words.
   This poem follows the AABB scheme.
   This poem describes feelings.
E. (Individual writing)

6 The Butterfly's Life Cycle

A. 4 ; 3 ; 1 ; 2
B. 1. a caterpillar
   2. a pupa
   3. a pupa
   4.
C. 1. The Butterfly's Life Cycle
   2. It is about the life cycle of a butterfly.
   3. There are four pictures. They show the four stages in the life cycle of a butterfly.

Answers — Section 4

D. (Suggested diagram)

Title: The Butterfly's Life Cycle

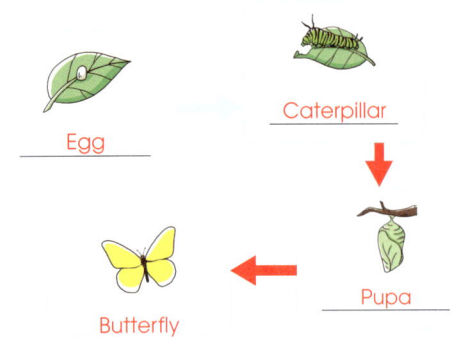

Egg → Caterpillar → Pupa → Butterfly

(Check these characteristics.)
arrows ; text ; title ; color ; labels ; pictures

E. (Individual diagram)

7 Crispy Squares

A. 2 ; 3 ; 4 ; 1

B. 1. Step 1
   2. measuring cup
   3. a kitchen tool
   4. 🥚

C. 1. It provides instructions on how to make crispy squares.
   2. Rice crispies, marshmallows, and margarine are needed.
   3. It is used for stirring the marshmallows into the margarine.

D. Smoothie
   Ingredients: 4 strawberries ; 2 ice cubes ; 1 peeled banana ; 1 cup of milk
   Utensils: measuring cup ; glass ; blender
   Directions:
   1. Put all the ingredients into the blender.
   2. Blend them for one minute.
   3. Pour the smoothie into a glass.

E. (Individual drawing and writing)

8 Jumbo the Gigantic Elephant

A. 1. jumbe – chief
   2. almost – nearly
   3. enormous – very big
   4. star – famous performer

B. 1. Victoria
   2. Swahili
   3. Jumbo
   4. 🎪

C. 1. Jumbo was kept at the London Zoo in the early 1880s.
   2. He could carry up to 100 children.
   3. A zookeeper of the London Zoo gave Jumbo his name.

D. Date of the Accident: September 15, 1885
   Place of the Accident: St. Thomas ; Ontario ; Canada
   Whom Jumbo Wanted to Save: Tom Thumb
   What Jumbo Was Struck by: a train
   When Jumbo's Statue Was Erected: in 1985
   Where Jumbo's Statue Was Erected: in St. Thomas

E. (Individual answers and drawing)

9 Bat Facts

A. 1. ✔   2.
   3. ✔   4. ✔
   5.

B. 1. not very hot or cold
   2. its hearing
   3. at night
   4. 🪲 ; 🍌

C. 1. It contains facts.
   2. The subheadings are "Habitat," "Diet," and "Senses."
   3. They give birth to live young.

Answers

Section 4 — Grade 2

D. A bat flies at night without crashing. ~~This is because bats are magical animals.~~ It makes noise and listens for it to bounce back. This noise is called an echo. ~~An echo is created by an enchanted wand.~~ The echo tells a bat where an object is. Then the bat can avoid the object. ~~That is why no bats have crashed into the witch's castle.~~

A bat flies at night without crashing. It makes noise and listens for it to bounce back. This noise is called an echo. The echo tells a bat where an object is. Then the bat can avoid the object.

E. (Individual writing and drawing)

10 Big Red Rescuer

A. (Check these features.)
has light ; has a hose ; battery-operated ; is red ; has sound ; has an extendable ladder

B. 1. water
2. a toy truck
3. save
4.

C. 1. It is promoting a toy fire truck.
2. The audience is kids and parents.
3. Some words are in bold to catch the audience's attention.

D. 1. superwoman costume
2. parents ; young girls
3. to persuade
4. Be a Superwoman!
5. $15.99
6. B
7. B

E. (Individual answers and design)

Review 4

A. 1. characters
2. before, after, then
3. A folktale
4. the sender's
5. addresses and a stamp
6. paragraphs
7. first ; second
8. a poem
9. graphic text
10. labels and pictures
11.
12. step-by-step instructions
13. contains fictional information
14. different subheadings
15. an ad

B. 1. ✔
2. ✘
3. ✘
4. ✔
5. ✔

C. 1. It is an informational text.
2. It helps spread pollen from one plant to another.
3. It makes honey by chewing the pollen and mixing it with its saliva.
4. (Individual answer)

D.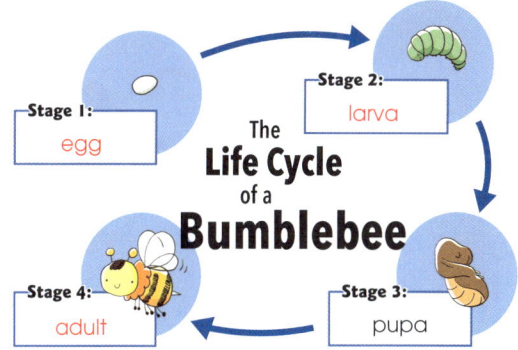

(Individual writing)

E. (Individual writing and design)

Answers

Language Games

1.
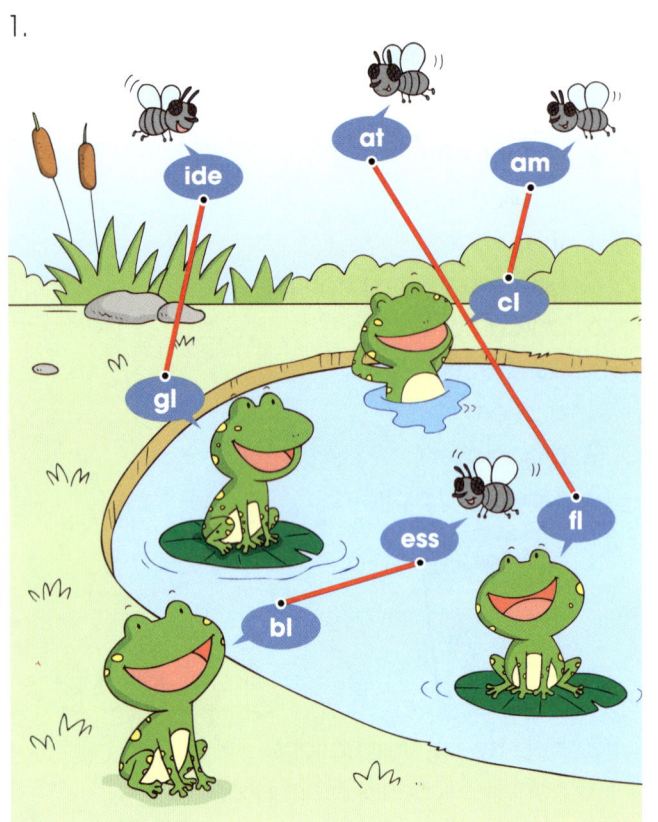

2.
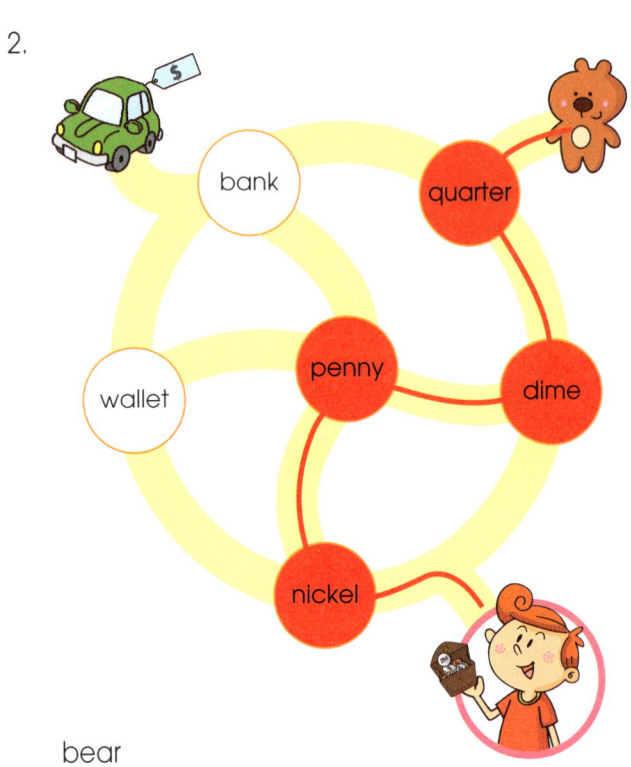

3.

4.

Answers
Language Games — Grade 2

5.

6. A. duckling
   B. puppy
   C. calf
   D. fawn
   E. piglet
   F. cub

7.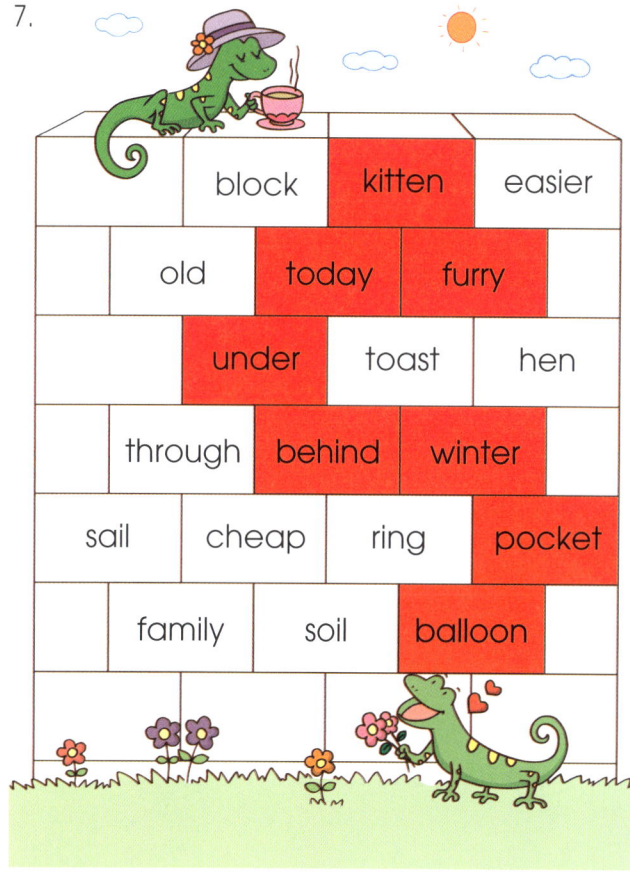

8. (Color the rhyming pairs with the same color.)
   dim – swim
   dot – spot
   ink – pink
   bake – cake
   walk – talk

Complete English Success (Grade 2)

Answers

Language Games

9.

10.

11. (Color the eggs with these words.)
    den ; ten ; men ; pen ; Ben
12. (Individual drawing)
    1. cat
    2. rabbit/bunny
    3. fish
    4. octopus
    5. snake
13.

Language Games

Language Games — **Phonics – Consonant Blends**

1 Draw a line to connect each frog to a fly to form a word.

Language Games | Vocabulary – Coin Words

2 Color the coins that have coin words on them. Then draw a line to help Julian buy his favorite toy and fill in the blank.

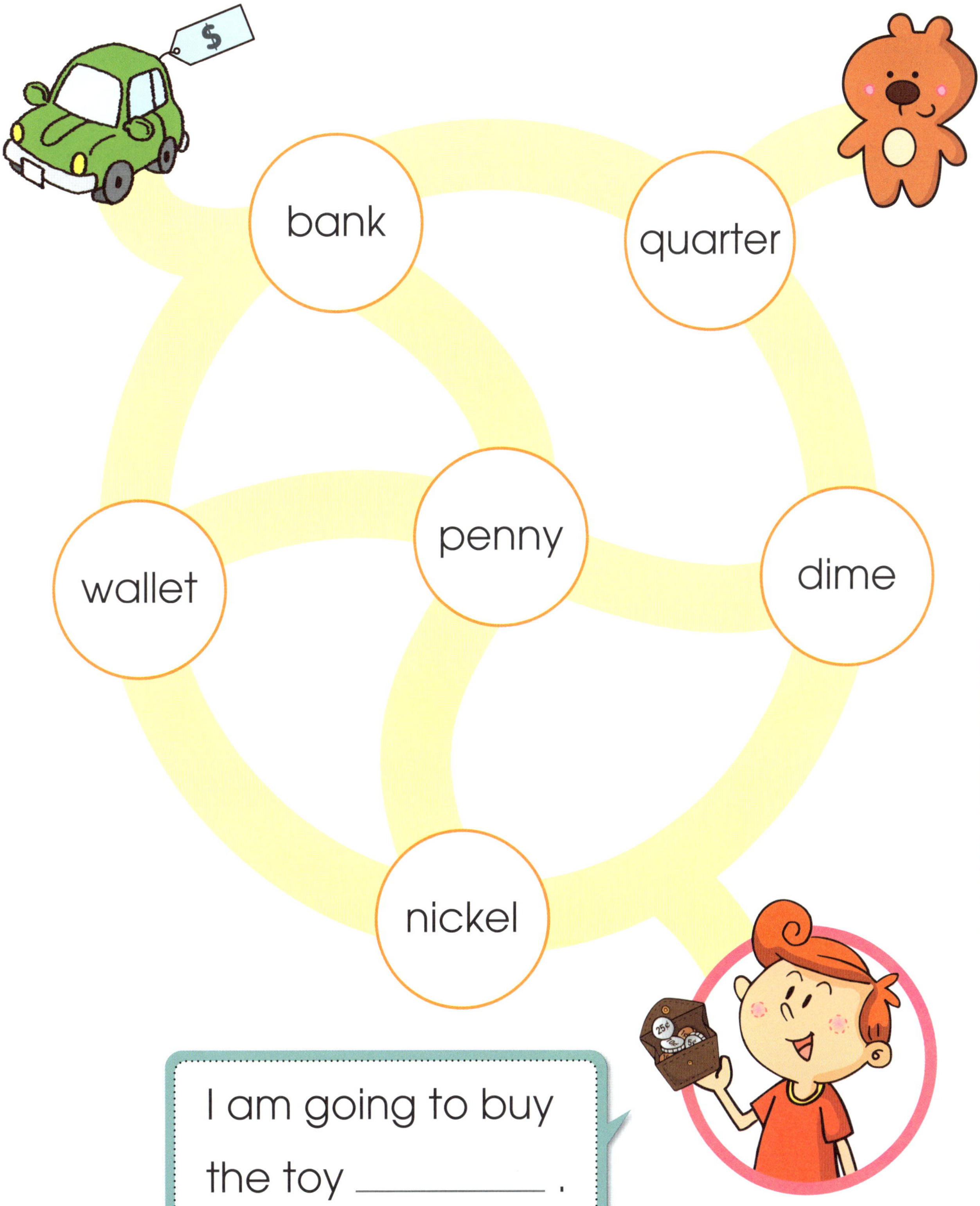

- bank
- quarter
- penny
- wallet
- dime
- nickel

I am going to buy the toy _____ .

Language Games — Vocabulary – Beach Words

3 Complete the crossword puzzle with the beach words.

umbrella sea
pail shell
spade sun
hat seagull

Language Games — Phonics – Consonants

4 Color the fish with consonants on them to bring Casey Cat to the mermaid.

Hi, Casey!

Language Games — Vocabulary – Pet Words

5 Read the clues and complete the crossword puzzle.

Across

- **A** This pet likes to run on a turning wheel.
- **B** A canary is one.
- **C** This pet may be named Porky.
- **D** If your pet rabbit was named King Rabbitoh, what would its initials be?
- **E** another word for "rabbit"
- **F** A bird's claws are its _____ .

Down

1. what pet cats like to drink
2. another word for "bunny"
3. Rabbits like to twitch their _____ .
4. A pet frog or a pet snake may lay these.
5. We keep these in a bowl or tank.
6. This pet has been called "Man's Best Friend."

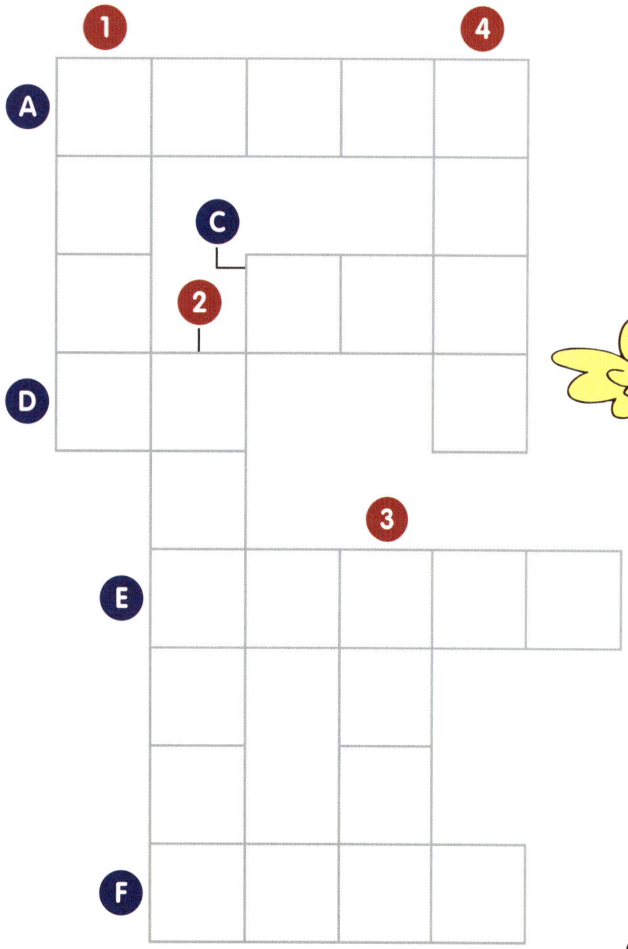

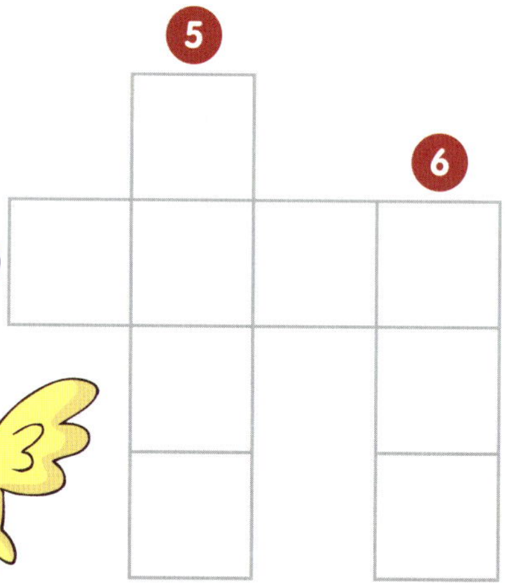

Language Games **Vocabulary – Baby Animal Words**

6 Look at the shadows of the baby animals. Write what they are. Then write the letters in the circles.

duckling   cub
fawn   piglet
puppy   calf

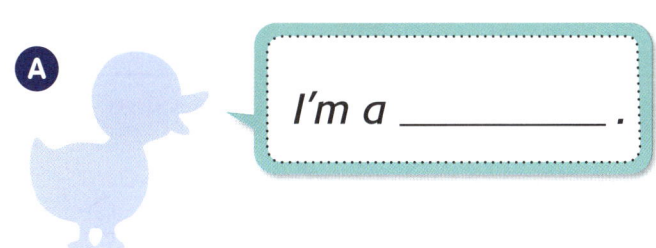
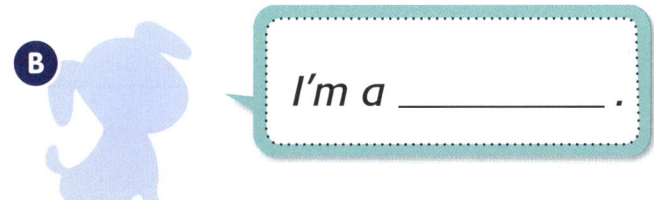
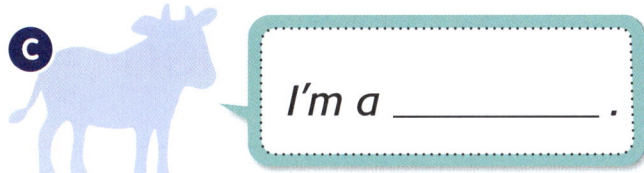
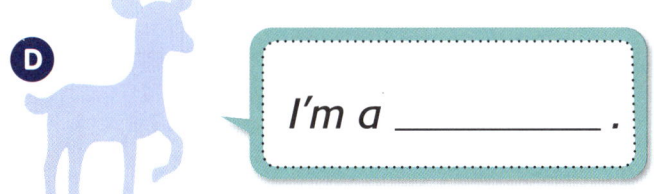
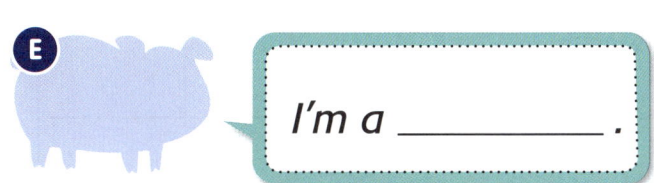
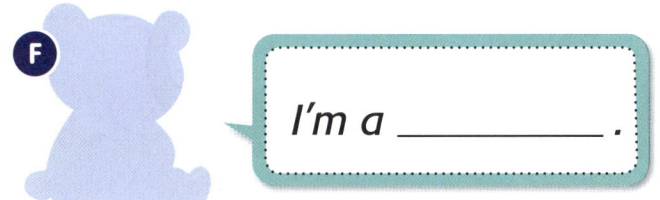

Language Games — **Phonics – Two-syllable Words**

7 Help Leo the Lizard find his way up the wall by coloring the two-syllable words.

	block	kitten	easier
old	today	furry	
	under	toast	hen
through	behind	winter	
sail	cheap	ring	pocket
family	soil	balloon	

266 Complete English Success (Grade 2)

Language Games — Rhyming Words

8 Help the animals find their eggs by coloring each rhyming pair with the same color.

- dim
- dot
- ink
- bake
- spot
- walk
- swim
- cake
- pink
- talk

Language Games — Vocabulary – Animal Words

9 Circle the animal words in the word search.

duck	sheep	horse	goat	pig
dog	goose	turkey		
rabbit	cow	chicken	pigeon	

```
      s  y  a  n  p
   c  s  h  e  e  p  g  s  o
   g  e  t  o  x  h  l  w  b  c  e
p  i  a  c  b  p  s  k  j  r  v  p
c  d  g  l  j  g  d  g  o  a  t  i  n
h  o  r  s  e  z  w  o  i  b  n  g  d
r  g  d  h  x  t  q  o  u  b  k  e  i
k  n  j  m  d  u  y  s  p  i  g  o  b
b  o  a  v  u  r  h  e  z  t  y  n  h
l  c  h  i  c  k  e  n  v  s  o  r  c
e  j  f  e  k  e  q  r  t  a        a
z  u  x  v  i  y  m  c  o  w     x  r
a  c  v  e  r        w  f  n  i     s  d
```

268 Complete English Success (Grade 2)

Language Games — Vocabulary – Animal Words

10 Unscramble the letters to write the names of the animals.

- frafeig
- ilon
- theeplan 
- rogllai
- nkmoey
- npada

Language Games | **Rhyming Words**

11 Help Mother Hen find her eggs by coloring the eggs that rhyme with "hen."

Where are they?

- den
- men
- fan
- ten
- mean
- pen
- lend
- Ben
- send
- mend

Complete English Success (Grade 2)

Language Games | **Vocabulary – Animal Words**

12 Draw to complete the animal stickers. Then write their names in the boxes.

My Sticker Sheet

1.
2.
3.
4.
5.

Language Games — Vocabulary – Color Words

13 Find and circle the color words in the word search. Then color them the correct colors.

b	p	e	j	p	u	r	p	l	e	b
c	i	p	g	r	e	e	n	i	d	r
f	n	s	l	c	y	s	o	a	f	o
j	k	o	a	t	e	m	e	y	t	w
b	o	r	v	h	l	b	l	u	e	n
l	r	a	b	z	l	w	d	i		
a	i	n	m	x	o	z	o	z		
c	d	g	e	p	w	q				
k	a	e	h	b	j	f	a			
g	r	e	d	w	h	i	t	e		

272   Complete English Success (Grade 2)